Activism and Rhetc

Activism and Rhetoric examines the role of rhetoric in today's culture of democratic activism. The essays included herein enact a wide range of activist experiences and commitments, as well as an array of political positions and presentational styles. The volume tackles two of the most significant challenges currently facing contemporary rhetorical studies: (1) the contested meanings and practices of democracy and civic engagement in global context, and (2) the central role of rhetoric in democratic activist practices. In presenting a variety of political and rhetorical struggles in their specific contexts, editors Seth Khan and JongHwa Lee allow contributors to reflect on and elaborate possibilities for both activist approaches to rhetorical studies, and rhetorical approaches to activist projects, facilitating better understanding of the socio-political consequences of this work.

With contributions from widely known scholars in communication and composition studies, this collection offers practical cases that highlight how rhetoric mediates, constitutes, and/or intervenes in democratic principles and practices. It also considers theoretical questions that acknowledge profound voids in the rhetorical tradition (e.g., Western, neo-Aristotelian, liberal) and expand the horizon of traditional rhetorical perspectives. It advocates new knowledge and practices that further promote civic engagement, social change, and democracy in the global context.

Activism and Rhetoric is appropriate for scholars and students across disciplines, including rhetoric, composition, communication studies, political science, cultural studies, and women's studies.

Seth Kahn, Ph.D., is Associate Professor of English at West Chester University of Pennsylvania, where he teaches writing and rhetoric courses, and serves in several positions for APSCUF (Association of PA State College University Faculty). His current research projects are focused on the term "shared governance" and its availability to higher education labor activists as a means to reclaim some authority over our own work.

JongHwa Lee, Ph.D., is an Assistant Professor of Communication Studies at Loyola Marymount University. He teaches courses on the rhetoric of human rights and human wrongs, tourism and globalization, and the rhetoric of memory and space. He was the chief organizer of the World Conference on Japanese Military Sexual Slavery held in University of California at Los Angeles in 2007.

Contents

List of Boxes

Chapter 1
What Is Research and Why We Do It

This chapter sets the stage for what is presented in the rest of the book. It discusses the notions of *science* and *scientific research* in Sects. 1.1 and 1.2, and analyzes the motivations for doing research. Exploring the unknown has always been a profound human aspiration. Whenever humans reach the boundaries of knowledge, they try to push them further. Generation of new knowledge, however, is not only a purely intellectual endeavor. As we discuss in Sect. 1.3, new knowledge ignites human progress and societal innovations.

To understand and appreciate the role of scientific research in human society, we need to realize that research is not a monolithic sector, but instead it is a complex and highly diversified system in which different areas of knowledge are investigated and different intellectual approaches coexist and fertilize each other. Diversity is key to research, as we discuss over and over throughout this book. Section 1.4 looks at this problem by discussing the blurred boundaries—or continuity and complementarity—between *research* and *applications of research* and the possible different categories in which research endeavors may be classified. Section 1.5 gives a closer look to how research is embedded in society: how research impacts on society and how society drives and supports research. Finally, Sect. 1.6 focuses on the specific role of research in Informatics. This role is especially crucial, since Informatics is driving the current move towards the creation of the digital society in which we live, which is generating new and unprecedented changes that are re-shaping the world in the third millennium.

1.1 What Is Science

The notion of science has been debated by scientists and philosophers for centuries and its meaning has evolved over time. In this book, the term science (from Latin "scientia", meaning "knowledge") is used to indicate a systematically organized body of knowledge on a particular subject. According to this definition, there are

© Springer Nature Switzerland AG 2020

C. Ghezzi, *Being a Researcher*, https://doi.org/10.1007/978-3-030-45157-8_1

Table 1.1 Social Sciences
and Humanities

Social Sciences and Humanities	
SH1	Individuals, Markets and Organisations
SH2	Institutions, Values, Beliefs and Behaviour
SH3	The Social World, Diversity, Population
SH4	The Human Mind and Its Complexity
SH5	Cultures and Cultural Production
SH6	The Study of the Human Past

Table 1.2 Life Sciences

Life Sciences	
LS1	Molecular and Structural Biology and Biochemistry
LS2	Genetics, Genomics, Bioinformatics and Systems Biology
LS3	Cellular and Developmental Biology
LS4	Physiology, Pathophysiology and Endocrinology
LS5	Neuroscience and Neural Disorders
LS6	Immunity and Infection
LS7	Diagnostic Tools, Therapies and Public Health
LS8	Evolutionary, Population and Environmental Biology
LS9	Applied Life Sciences and Non-Medical Biotechnology

as many sciences as there are subjects. Natural sciences study natural phenomena; physical sciences, which study non-living systems, are part of natural sciences, as are life sciences. Social sciences study the social life of individuals and human groups, while psychology studies the human mind and its functions affecting behavior in given contexts. Informatics (also known as Computer Science) is the research area on which this book is mostly focused. It is much younger than most other sciences, which have a longer tradition. Informatics is the science that studies algorithmic methods for computing, their application and interaction in natural and artificial systems.

Sciences can be classified in different ways and for different purposes. A classification is often hierarchical, to highlight the refinement of large and general categories into more specialized ones. A possible taxonomy is the one adopted by the European Research Council for research funding purposes. It is summarized in Tables 1.1, 1.2, 1.3 for Social Sciences and Humanities (SH), Life Sciences (LS), and Physical Sciences and Engineering (PE), respectively.

SH includes Social Sciences, which study people and societies; Humanities, which study humans in their historical, cultural, political context, and Economic Sciences, which study the economic behavior of individuals and societies. LS spans from Biology to Genetics to Medical Sciences and Public Health, to Ecology and Evolution. PE spans from Physics to Informatics to Products and Process Engineering to Earth Sciences.

In this taxonomy, *engineering* is rightly considered as a part of science. Indeed, it is the branch concerned with the invention, design, construction, and use of new products, processes, and methods. Sometimes, science and engineering are instead

Table 1.3 Physical Sciences and Engineering

Physical Sciences and Engineering	
PE1	Mathematics
PE2	Fundamental Constituents of Matter
PE3	Condensed Matter Physics
PE4	Physical and Analytical Chemical Sciences
PE5	Synthetic Chemistry and Materials
PE6	Computer Science and Informatics
PE7	Systems and Communication Engineering
PE8	Products and Processes Engineering
PE9	Universe Sciences
PE10	Earth System Science

kept separate, and the latter is viewed as the mere application of the former. A distinction is also often made between *science* and *technology*. The term technology comes from Greek, "techne" (skill). Technology can be defined as the systematically organized study of techniques, methods, and processes used in the production of goods or services and the accomplishment of specific objectives for the benefit of humans, often through machines or other kinds of automated entities. Technology is science driven by practical motivations and finalized to development of applicable solutions. A reductive view considers technology as the application of science in a particular area for practical uses.

Yet another distinction is sometimes made between *basic* (also called *pure*, or *fundamental*) and *applied* science. Sometimes the terms *curiosity-driven* and *practice-driven* are also used to draw the distinction. Basic research is far-looking, while applied research looks for shorter-term results. The former has a high risk of failure to deliver significant results, while the latter is less risky. The term "pure" is used to indicate non-contamination by mundane practical ends. As our discussions will show, these distinctions are often fuzzy and should not be used to draw strict boundaries where in reality a continuity exists. Even worse, sometimes distinctions are made as a form of snobbism that draws a class distinction within different approaches to science.[1] Separating science from engineering (or technology), or fundamental science from applied science is becoming increasingly impossible, useless, and even counterproductive. A variety of approaches indeed exists, which goes much beyond a binary distinction, and all approaches can be equally valuable and respectable. By crystallizing sharp distinctions among them into different categories we would only fail to capture continuity of approaches and their increasing amalgamation. Variety and diversity make science a rich, vibrant, and vital sector.

---

[1] In [34], P.E. Medawar discusses what he calls the "snobismus" of pure versus applied science. In his words, this is one of the most damaging forms of snobbism, which draws a class distinction between pure and applied science.

1.2   What Is Scientific Research

According to the OECD Frascati Manual [37], research comprises "creative and systematic work undertaken in order to increase the stock of knowledge—including knowledge of humankind, culture and society—and to devise new applications of available knowledge." This book is mainly concerned with *scientific and technological research*, that is research that covers the whole spectrum—from production and delivery of new theoretical scientific results and generation of new knowledge, to the development of new solutions of standing societal and industrial problems, to innovation of existing practices.

Looking at the definition, I would like to stress that research has to be both *creative* and *systematic*, in order to lead to an increase of the stock of knowledge or to devising new applications of human knowledge. Creativity is the skill that may lead to discovery of original, novel results. But creativity must be sustained by systematic approaches that make the results also rigorous and significant. Originality is what causes an increase of the stock of knowledge. The novel results produced by research must be the ultimate outputs of a rigorous process, which assures their validity. The work has also to be significant, otherwise it would not generate knowledge or new solutions, but just ephemeral or irrelevant outputs. This can be summarized by saying that the essential ingredients of scientific research are:

- *originality*;
- *rigor*;
- *significance*.[2]

Let us dig a bit more into these important concepts: *Originality* means that the results of the research are novel: they were not known before. The results may be specific new findings or even new ways of thinking about a subject or new and better ways of achieving known solutions. The results may state new laws of nature, show new mathematical theorems, or describe new ways of doing things.

Rigor refers to the intellectual integrity of the research process and the way the results are demonstrated. It is understood in terms of the intellectual precision, robustness, and appropriateness of the concepts and methods adopted within the outcome. In the case of empirical research, this refers to the way experimental data are collected and analyzed. For other kinds of research, it may refer to the rigor of mathematical treatment.

Significance means that research has *intellectual depth*. Its outcomes exert, or have the potential to exert, an influence—on society, industry, or other research. It is a multi-faceted concept. An outcome may be significant because it solves a

---

[2]Originality, rigor, and significance have been defined and used as the key criteria to evaluate research outputs by the UK Research Excellence Framework (REF) [46]. A research evaluation exercise has been performed periodically since 1986 on UK higher education institutions and their research outputs have been rated according to their originality, rigor, and significance.

difficult open problem that is deemed important by society. It may be significant because the scientific community views it as an open challenge. It may be significant because the creative process behind the research was especially demanding, or because of the degree of uncertainty that was initially attributed to the problem addressed by the research. It may also be significant because it leads to significant practical improvement in the way certain things used to be done before its invention. Significance can thus span a wide spectrum of characteristics: from purely theoretical to very practical (e.g., a new process that causes significant cost reduction). Significance may be judged differently according to the domain in which research is performed (for example, in the context of theoretical science versus engineering) or the organization hosting and supporting research (for example, academia versus industry). In any case, however, significance has to do with the ability of a research to be transferred, for example to other research efforts or to practical use, or to be reproducible in other contexts and/or by other people.

Significance of a research is generally harder to assess than originality and rigor. The potential impact of a given research may in fact take time to manifest itself. It is also important to observe that originality, rigor, and significance are not binary attributes. They are measured over a continuous scale of values. Not all research produced by researchers scores high on all three dimensions. A research can be exceptionally important and lead its authors to be awarded the Nobel Prize (for example, for Physics or Chemistry), or the Turing Award (for Informatics), or the Field Medal (for Mathematics). These, however, are the exceptional cases that deserve the highest honors of recognition in their respective fields. A research can just be very good and be recognized as such by its specific research community. Or it can simply be solid and useful work without reaching any special peak in either originality, rigor, or significance. However, a certain degree of originality, significance, and rigor is expected to be met by any result that can be qualified as a contribution to the advancement of science. The threshold is not carved in stone or in any research recipe book, but is rather agreed upon *socially* by the research community. Originality, rigor, and significance are the key criteria researchers should constantly use to guide and self-assess their work and assess the work by others. As discussed in this book, they are the cornerstone principles of research evaluation.

1.3   Why Do We Do Research?

Research aims at discovering new knowledge. It is largely driven by human curiosity. The motivation to push knowledge beyond the boundary of what is currently known is intrinsic in human nature and has led humans to dominate the world. Dante's compelling words attributed to Ulysses:

> Fatti non foste a viver come bruti ma per seguir virtute e canoscenza
> (Ye were not form'd to live the life of brutes, but virtue to pursue and knowledge high.)
> (The Divine Comedy - Inferno, Canto 26)

carved this concept into immortal poetry.

Scientific research, however, is not just an irrepressible human aspiration. Humans discovered that it has also been the main driving force that generated progress of human society. They discovered that the new knowledge acquired through research has led them to progress and gave them the power to dominate the world. In his fascinating book "Sapiens—A Brief History of Human Kind" [19], Y. N. Harari wrote a chapter on "The Scientific Revolution", where he observes that the last 500 years have witnessed a phenomenal and unprecedented growth in human power, mainly due to scientific research. Quoting from [19]:

> During the last five centuries, humans increasingly came to believe that they could increase their capabilities by investing in scientific research. This wasn't just blind faith—it was repeatedly proven empirically. The more proofs there were, the more resources wealthy people and governments were willing to put into science.

Harari's point can be summarized by the feedback loop illustrated in Fig. 1.1. The figure shows that research empowers society and generates resources that, in turn, can be invested to produce further research. History taught us that to sustain human progress, the human aspiration to generate new knowledge must be fueled by continuously investing new resources. Research is not an optional luxury niche of society, rather it is the engine that drives society to progress and growth. Sometimes the positive feedback loop is countered by short-sighted political motivations, especially in periods of economic difficulties. By reducing support to research, however, progress is endangered, and this may further exacerbate the economic difficulties.

Another way of looking at the relation between research and society is illustrated by Fig. 1.2, which shows the endless flow of research: almost inevitably, research generates further research, both directly and indirectly. The flow is the result of a collective effort, to which all scientists contribute, at different levels. Research directly generates new research that may improve previous results, or remedy failure of previous attempts. An example of directly self-feeding research flow is histori-

Fig. 1.1 Research and society

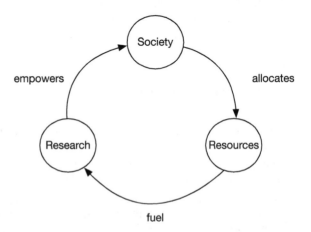

cally represented by advances in steam engine technology—see Box 1.1—which generated the industrial revolution in the eighteenth and nineteenth centuries. As another example, software failures generated a lot of research and new developments in programming languages in the last decades of the past century—see Box 1.2.

Research can also generate further research indirectly, typically by inspiring the birth of a new research thread in a new field. An example is briefly illustrated in Box 1.3, which shows that research in Linguistics led to original research in Informatics. Compilers are widely used software tools which perform automatic translation of programs written in a high-level programming language into code executable by computers. Compiler technology is based on a theory that was inspired by research in Linguistics.

The scientific revolution occurred between the mid sixteenth century and the end of the seventeenth century, with the work of giants like Francis Bacon, Nicolaus Copernicus, Johannes Kepler, Galileo Galilei, René Descartes, and Isaac Newton. Some of their foundational contributions will be discussed in Chap. 2. Their work changed what was previously considered to be science into our modern view. According to Harari [19], the modern view differs from previous traditional knowledge in three fundamental aspects:

1. *The willingness to admit ignorance.* Modern science assumes that we don't know everything. It even accepts that things that we think we know can be proven wrong as we gain new knowledge.[3]
2. *The centrality of observation and mathematics.* Modern science is based on these two pillars: gather observations through experiments and use mathematics to explain, connect, systematize, and generalize. Mathematics abstracts observations into *theories*.
3. *The effort to transform knowledge into power.* Modern science uses these theories to empower humans, and in particular to develop new technologies. This approach shows the benefit of not viewing science and technology as a dichotomy, but rather as a continuous spectrum of endeavors.

It is important to stress that mere observations per-se do not lead to new knowledge. In order to understand phenomena, we need to connect observations into

Fig. 1.2 Scientific revolution's feedback

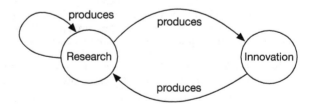

---

[3]The importance of realizing that "we don't know" was apparently first stated by Socrates, according to Plato's account of his thought. This is condensed in the famous paradox "I know that I don't know."

Box 1.1: Steam Engines

The invention of steam-powered engines is often cited as the enabling factor of the industrial revolution, which progressively replaced human labor with machines, generating the transition to the new manufacturing industry in the eighteenth and nineteenth centuries. The first steam-powered device was a water pump, developed in 1698 by Thomas Savery to mechanize the mining industry in the UK. The first piston steam engine was developed about 10 years after. A sequence of research contributions and major technological improvements occurred since. Progress was made under the pressure to mitigate the often experienced risks of explosion and at the same time produce high-pressure engines. Advances led to expanding the use of steam-powered engines to produce automation in many sectors: from the textile industry to railways, from the initial road vehicles to the steam turbines used for ship propulsion or for producing electricity.

In one of early scientific contributions to historical developments in steam engines [59], Robert Henry Thurston reflected on the research efforts that led to technological progress and came to the following conclusion, which is still valid today:

> Great inventions are never, and great discoveries are seldom, the work of any one mind. Every great invention is really an aggregation of minor inventions, or the final step of a progression. It is not usually a creation, but a growth, as truly so as is the growth of the trees in the forest.

comprehensive theories. Earlier traditions usually formulated their theories in terms of stories or myths. Modern science uses mathematics. Quoting again Harari [19],

> there are very few equations, graphs and calculations in the Bible, the Qur'an, the Vedas or the Confucian classics. When traditional mythologies and scriptures laid down general laws, these were presented in narrative rather than mathematical form. Thus a fundamental principle of Manichaean religion asserted that the world is a battleground between good and evil. An evil force created matter, while a good force created spirit. Humans are caught between these two forces, and should choose good over evil. Yet the prophet Mani made no attempt to offer a mathematical formula that could be used to predict human choices by quantifying the respective strength of these two forces. He never calculated that "the force acting on a man is equal to the acceleration of his spirit divided by the mass of his body."

Scientists formulate theories grounded on mathematics, which can be used to explain and predict phenomena.[4] Isaac Newton's general theory of movement, which explains and predicts the movements of bodies in space, was published in 1687 in a book titled *The Mathematical Principles of Natural Philosophy*. Although almost three centuries later this theory was challenged by new observations and

---

[4]This view applies mainly to natural and physical sciences.

Box 1.2: Programming Languages

At the end of the 1970s, the diffusion of software applications to automate many sectors of society was accompanied by numerous manifestations of alarming failures. It became clear that many of the software bugs that caused these failures could have been spotted by automatically analyzing programs, before executing them in the real world. This, however, required writing the program in a language that enforced certain rules and restrictions.

A famous case, which shocked the public in 1962, was the failure of Mariner 1, designed for exploration of Venus. Shortly after takeoff the rocket responded improperly to commands from the guidance systems on the ground, due to a software error. Apparently this error was due to a simple statement, like:

$$DO15I = 1.100 \tag{1.1}$$

which was intended to express 100 iterations of a code fragment. Unfortunately, to be interpreted as an iteration, the statement should have been written as:

$$DO15I = 1, 100 \tag{1.2}$$

Writing a period instead of a comma caused the compiler to interpret the statement as the (useless) assignment of the real number 1.1 to a variable called $DO15I$, thus not executing the required iteration. In fact, the language in which the program was written (FORTRAN), automatically interpreted $DO15I$ as the name of a new assignable floating point variable. Should the language have explicitly required that all variables used in a program must be explicitly declared along with their type, the error would have been caught by the compiler.

Other alarming cases were security violations, where malicious code was injected and then executed without any explicit permission. This was possible in programs written in the widely used C language, due to its ability to allow free access to any area of memory through *pointers*.

Software failures led researchers to study new programming languages that would favor writing reliable software, by supporting early error detection, without requiring programs to be executed. For example, this research led to the development of now widely used strongly-typed *object-oriented languages*, like *Java*, which allow detection of data manipulation errors by the compiler, before generating executable code.

Box 1.3: Linguistics and Informatics

In the 1960s the field of linguistics was highly influenced by the work by A.N. Chomsky, whose research focused on understanding the structure of language. He postulated that humans are all born with an innate knowledge of grammar, which serves as the basis for language acquisition. He introduced the concept of a *generative grammar*, which dictates the syntax of sentences and consists of a limited number of rules, expressible in a mathematical notation. Chomsky introduced a hierarchy of classes of formal grammars: regular (or Type-3) grammars, context-free (or Type-2) grammars, context-sensitive (or Type-1) grammars, and unrestricted (or Type-0) grammars. Informatics researchers showed that programming languages can be described by context-free grammars, and that the translation of programs written in a programming language into equivalent code executable by a computer can be systematically and even semi-automatically built based on the language's grammar.

The Chomsky hierarchy became also a foundation for theoretical computer science research, along with automata theory and the theory of computation [22]. In particular, the languages generated by a Type-3 grammar were shown to be recognizable by finite-state automata, while the languages generated by Type-0 grammar are recognizable by Turing machines.

As a side remark, we notice that Informatics also had a profound influence on linguistics, in particular on automatic translation from one natural language to another. Machine learning techniques are increasingly used successfully by computational linguists to improve accuracy of automatic translation of natural languages.

---

new theories were formulated (relativity theory and quantum mechanics), Newton's theory still provides an adequate explanation in most practical settings. The theory can be used to predict the behavior of moving bodies, and machines can be designed, whose behaviors are accurately described by the theory.

Starting from the seventeenth century, scientists have learned to develop theories and mathematically describe them. As mentioned earlier, precisely formulated scientific knowledge empowered humans to build *predictable artifacts* through *predictable processes* in all fields. For example, the theory of thermodynamics helped develop better and more reliable steam engines.

The first formulation of the concept that "knowledge is power" ("Scientia potentia est") is attributed to Francis Bacon. In a modern interpretation, the knowledge generated by scientific research is not just something we discover to be true for intellectual fulfillment. It is something that empowers humans and allows society to progress. Our discussion also shows that in most cases a valuable result of scientific research (new knowledge) is not the discovery of something that is correct in absolute terms. A result may hold only under certain specific restrictions. For example, Newton's laws explain and predict very accurately the motion of bodies, only at non-relativistic speeds. This restriction holds in most practical cases, and makes Newton's laws perfectly adequate in everyday's life. They are extremely useful and have empowered society immensely.

1.4 Different Kinds of Research

I already mentioned that scientific research hosts a variety of different approaches, all legitimately contributing to its fertility and potentially generating progress. Understanding and acknowledging diversity, however, does not mean that research and researchers should be isolated into separate silos that do not communicate. Different approaches can be appropriate for different research targets, and often they co-exist in the same research activity by a researcher. Moreover, researchers may change focus and may be engaged in different kinds of research at different times.

This section explores the variety of possible research approaches. The exploration does not aim at an exhaustive coverage, which would simply be impossible. Rather, it tries to shed light on the richness of possible, equally legitimate and respectable, ways of doing research.

We already saw a possible difference between basic and applied research (and between science and technology), which often leads to heated and controversial discussions about their distinctive features and merits. The distinction was raised very clearly and became current at the end of World War II. The war was a worldwide tragedy, but at the same time it was a spectacular showcase of the fundamental role of research in empowering the defensive and offensive power of different countries. For example, the Manhattan Project financed by the USA government led to the development of the nuclear bomb that ended the war. After the war ended, USA president Roosevelt asked Vannevar Bush, head of the Office of Scientific Research Development during war, to advise him on the role of research during peace. Bush produced a report in 1945, titled "Science, the Endless Frontier", which not only influenced the future developments and funding initiatives in the USA, but also had a deep influence on the research policies adopted in other parts of the post-war world. Among other things, Bush called for continuous government support for science and pressed for the creation of the USA National Science Foundation.

Bush introduced the term *basic research*. He defined it to indicate research "performed without thought of practical end." Basic research contributes to knowledge: its objective is to understand nature and its laws. According to Bush, the creativity needed to develop basic research would be lost if research were finalized to a premature attention to its practical usage. Basic research was thus contrasted with *applied research*. According to Bush, basic research is mainly *curiosity-driven*, long-term, theory-oriented, and has high risks of failing. Applied research is instead *problem-driven* and is more predictable. Its goal is to deliver potentially practical

basic research   applied research   development   production and operation

Fig. 1.3 Unidirectional flow of research into products according to Vannevar Bush (1945)

results. Applied research also includes what is sometimes called pre-competitive research, which aims at supporting the process of leading to innovative processes or products that can be produced by industry and, more generally, can give competitive advantage to companies or societies, supporting innovation.

According to Bush, basic research is the pacemaker of technological progress, and investments in it are needed for a society to be competitive. Bush saw a linear, waterfall-like progress from basic to applied research, and then to new development, production, and operation, where each of the successive stages depends upon the preceding one. The discoveries of basic research are taken up by applied research that makes discoveries exploitable; this leads to development of new products or processes, and eventually leads to production and operation (see Fig. 1.3).

This characterization is very idealistic. It does not provide an adequate account of the complexity that is intrinsic in today's scientific research and does not consider nor explain the variety of successful approaches that lead from research to innovations in society. The sequential research process shown in Fig. 1.3 does not capture the variety of situations that can influence and shape research endeavors. Basic research only driven by intellectual curiosity may have a fundamental role in expanding human knowledge, even when it does not lead to practical results in society. Most important, increasingly and almost inevitably, scientists find the motivations of their work in unsolved real-world problems. Fundamental research questions arise from the complexity of reality, from attempts to open new unexplored directions that may change people's life, or to try radically different solutions to traditional methods.

The research process is thus far from being linear. Rather, continuous feedback from the real world and from applications often drive the development of fundamentally explorative activities. Moreover, some purely speculative discoveries may not lead to any practical end, or they may do that unexpectedly after many years, perhaps in a completely unforeseen direction. Moshe Vardi refers to this phenomenon as "the long game of research" [63]. Because research is a long game, patience and endurance are necessary to play the game. He cites the so-called *Amara's Law*,[5] which says

> We tend to overestimate the effect of a technology in the short run and underestimate the effect in the long run.

Vardi also observes that research often progresses through landscapes, eloquently depicted as: the "peak of inflated expectations", corresponding to the phase in

---

[5]Roy Amara was President of the Institute for Future, a USA-based think tank, from 1971 until 1990.

which technology is overestimated, followed by the "trough of disillusionment", then the "slope of enlightenment", and finally, the "plateau of productivity", which progressively move from underestimation to proper appreciation. As an example, Vardi refers to Informatics research on deep neural networks, which generated a first storm of hype at the end of the 1960s and then again in the early 1980s. In the early 2000s, only a small group of scientists remained committed to this approach. Among those, Yoshua Bengio, Geoffrey Hinton, and Yann LeCun, who were later awarded the 2018 Turing Award[6] for "conceptual and engineering breakthroughs that have made deep neural networks a critical component of computing." Indeed, deep learning methods have been responsible for astonishing breakthroughs in many areas, like computer vision, speech recognition, natural language processing, and robotics.

The spectrum of possible research foci— ranging from fundamental to applied— is continuous. Open problems arising in the real world may be solved through more or less radically new and challenging research approaches. The distance from what is already known and what is attempted by research may also differ from case to case. The closer research goals are to current practice, the more likely research results will provide incremental practical benefits and gains. Incrementality leads to continuous, steady progress. Research may even aim primarily at delivering results that enhance competitiveness. By shifting more towards fundamental research foci, risks of failure are normally higher, although potential gains may also be higher. Risk management is thus an important aspect of research; it requires constantly assessing progress and possibly recalibrating objectives.

In conclusion, research is indeed a non-sequential and intrinsically iterative process. It proceeds through steps and decisions: choice of the problem to work on, expression of questions to be answered, formulation of hypotheses that may explain, development of theories or models, development of tools, design and execution of experiments. At any step, the researcher must be ready to step back and iterate, reformulating hypotheses and re-developing or refining previous decisions.

The spectrum of research motivations can range from pure intellectual curiosity to standing practical problems; its results can be more or less ready for practical usage. The separation line between basic and applied science is often blurred, as is the separation between science and technology (or between science and engineering). One can see a difference by examining the ends of the spectrum, but there is a continuum that connects them, with no precisely identifiable, discrete transition points.

Sometimes it is useful to refer to an additional, orthogonal set of categories that can be used to describe different approaches to research. Hereafter, I define them *research styles* and I briefly describe the main ones. Different styles can co-exist in a given research area and even in the same research. In particular, they are all present and relevant in Informatics.

---

[6]The Turing Award is generally recognized as the Nobel prize of Informatics.

Formal research is a research that studies a formal system. This is typically the case of a large part of research in mathematics, logic, statistics, systems theory, as well as in theoretical branches of computer science, information theory, microeconomics. Formal research mainly builds theories and models and proves theorems or produces simulations.

Analytic research instead observes and studies the world—nature, human artifacts and processes, humans, social groups, . . . , the universe—to build an organized knowledge in the form of theories, which provide explanations and predictions. Traditional and well-established examples of analytic research can be found in Physics, Chemistry, Biology, and Medicine. Newton's laws of motion and Darwin's theory of species' evolution and selection are examples of knowledge produced by analytic research. Experimental research is a fundamental component of analytic research. Experiments, in fact, inform and validate theories. Very often, when people refer to research, they implicitly refer to analytic research, assuming it to be the only kind of scientific inquiry. The discussion about scientific methods, which is the subject of Chap. 2, has also traditionally focused on the experimental component of analytic research.

Constructive research (sometimes also called *design research*) delivers concrete artifacts—new product prototypes, or new processes, or new methods—that can be considered as *proofs of concept*. The artifacts are constructed to show that a new kind of useful functionality can be produced. Research explains how artifacts may be built and predicts their behavior and use. Experiments play a fundamental role in artifact validation. Constructive research is very common in Engineering, where artifacts are mainly physical and processes occur in the physical world. It is also common very in Informatics, where artifacts are mainly digital.

A given research may span over more than one style. For example, it can have a formal science focus (development of a new theory) and a constructive focus (implementation of a new kind of tool). As another example, the theory developed by an analytic research can be subject to further purely mathematical investigations.

The presented taxonomy is not meant to provide an exhaustive coverage of research styles. For example, *action research* is an example of a research style that is often practiced in social sciences. It aims at driving personal or organizational change through processes that take action and same time collect observations that drive reflections on the actions.

1.5   Societal Impact of Research

Research generates new knowledge. New knowledge may produce *innovation*, through new products, methods, or processes, which can affect prosperity and generate progress in society and, ultimately, better living conditions for mankind. Because of the potential benefits of innovation, society supports the developments of research and tries to set up an eco-system that facilitates the transition from research to innovation. Financial support to research is part of the economic strategy of most

Table 1.4 Research investment by country (January 2020)

Country	%GDP spend	Total spend (US$ billions)	#Researchers/ MillionInhab.	%Female
Rep. Korea	4.3	73	6800	19
Israel	4.2	12	8250	–
Japan	3.4	170	5300	15
Switzerland	3.2	14	4450	32
Finland	3.2	7.2	7000	32
Sweden	3.1	14.2	6800	33
Austria	3.1	13	4900	30
Germany	2.9	110	4300	28
Denmark	2.9	7.8	7300	35
USA	2.7	476	4250	–
Belgium	2.4	12	4500	33
Slovenia	2.4	1.5	4100	36
France	2.3	61	4200	27
Australia	2.2	23	4500	–
Singapore	2.2	10	6700	30
China	2	370	1000	–
The Netherlands	2	16	4500	23
Czechia	2	7	3400	27
UK	1.7	44	4200	37
Canada	1.7	28	4500	–
Norway	1.7	5.8	5600	37

countries, mainly through public funding. According to UNESCO,[7] global spending on research has reached a record high of almost US$ 1.7 trillion. Table 1.4 reports data on the countries whose investments in research, measured as percentage of the GDP, exceed 1.5%. The situation worldwide is unfortunately very unbalanced: about ten countries account for 80% of spending. The data show that countries investing more in research also benefit tremendously in their economies as a result of major innovations.[8] The data also show that the research sector is still quite unbalanced in terms of gender.

An eco-system that facilitates transferring research into innovation involves three main entities: *government*, *industry*, and *academia*. Bilateral interactions between these entities are shown in Fig. 1.4. If they occur properly, they may foster and

---

[7] See http://uis.unesco.org/apps/visualisations/research-and-development-spending/.

[8] Israel is a very good example. Investments in research resulted in a proliferation of new, cutting-edge enterprises. The term *start-up nation* has been coined by Dan Senor and Saul Singer in their successful book [51] to characterize this phenomenon.

accelerate economic and social development. This is sometimes called the *Triple Helix* model [12].

Governments may interact with academia (and also industry) through *research funding*. They may do so by incentivizing research in certain priority areas where there is a special need and where potential societal benefits are expected. For example, the European Union, in consultation with stakeholders from industry, academia, and other sectors of society, issues multi-annual research programs and solicits researchers to apply for funding with proposals that focus on certain predefined themes. The themes are chosen according to their societal priority. The EU managed a research and innovation program—called Horizon 2020, covering seven years, from 2014 to 2020. This is an example of a *top-down* approach, which directs researchers to address selected relevant themes and only provides funding to work on them. It complements the classical *bottom-up* approach where researchers are free to propose research themes, purely based on their own intellectual interests, which are not necessarily driven by societal or industrial standing problems. More comments on top-down versus bottom-up research programs are given in Box 1.4, in the context of Horizon 2020.

Another fundamental mechanism is *human capital investment*. Governments and industry provide scholarships to students, who may be involved in research programs as PhD students or research assistants. Upon completion of their scholarship, those who move to industry or other sectors spread the new ideas they have been exposed to into the world.

Fig. 1.4 Triple Helix model

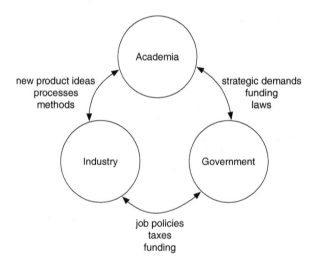

> ## Box 1.4: Top-Down Versus Bottom-Up Research Programs
>
> Hereafter I exemplify the distinction between top-down and bottom-up research programs by citing excerpts from the EU Horizon 2020 research and innovation program.[9] The program follows a typical top-down approach: it "reflects the policy priorities of the Europe 2020 strategy and addresses major concerns shared by citizens in Europe and elsewhere." The document specifies that funding should focus on the following challenges, reported verbatim:
>
> - Health, demographic change and wellbeing;
> - Food security, sustainable agriculture and forestry, marine and maritime and inland water research, and the bioeconomy;
> - Secure, clean and efficient energy;
> - Smart, green and integrated transport;
> - Climate action, environment, resource efficiency and raw materials;
> - Europe in a changing world—inclusive, innovative and reflective societies;
> - Secure societies—protecting freedom and security of Europe and its citizens.
>
> More specifically, for the period 2018–2020,[10] the following four areas are identified:
>
> - Building a low-carbon, climate resilient future;
> - Connecting economic and environmental gains—the circular economy;
> - Digitizing and transforming European industry and services;
> - Boosting the effectiveness of the Security Union.
>
> To complement these funding initiatives, the EU also supports bottom-up (or investigator-driven) research through the European Research Council—ERC. Researchers are free to apply for funding in any direction and field of research, rather than being led by priorities set by politicians. This ensures that funds are channelled into new and promising areas of research with a greater degree of flexibility.

Recognition and protection of *intellectual property rights* is another mechanism that is intended to support innovation. Governments play a fundamental role in their interaction with industry and academia in establishing intellectual property laws and enforcing them. This applies in particular to ownership of research inventions

---

[9]https://ec.europa.eu/programmes/horizon2020/en/h2020-section/societal-challenges.

[10]https://ec.europa.eu/programmes/horizon2020/en/h2020-section/cross-cutting-activities-focus-areas.

that produce novel artifacts—devices, methods, or processes. *Patents* are granted by national or regional patent offices. A patent right is granted in exchange for a public disclosure of the invention that enables its exploitation by others. A patent owner has the right to exclude others from making, using, selling, and importing the invention for a given period of time. Under agreements within the World Trade Organization's (WTO), patent policies are established and enforced in all its member states.

Different countries, however, may differ in the way patenting by researchers is regulated. For example, consider the typical case in which a researcher, who is a member of a research institution, is funded by a governmental agency through public money and the funded research leads to a patentable result: Who owns the right to patent? The research institution? The researcher? To facilitate transition from research to practical innovations, in several countries (for example, in the USA) research institutions are allowed to file, own, and license the intellectual property generated with government research funds. In this case, the researchers who originated the patent are often given a share of royalty revenue. In certain countries (for example, in Italy) the individual researchers own the rights of their inventions, but the research institution can handle the licensing to third parties and remunerate the owners.

The objective of a patent system is to incentivize research that can lead to exploitable inventions, to disclose them, and invest the money necessary to experiment, produce, and market them. It is fair to say, however, that there are also critical views, which claim that patents block innovation and waste resources (e.g., due to patent-related overheads and litigations) that could instead be invested in further advances.

Another mechanism to favor the transition from research to innovations consists in supporting academic entrepreneurship through *spin-offs*. Research institutions increasingly incentivize research groups to capitalize on their inventions by creating new companies that bring to the market the application of their scientific and technological inventions in new products, services, processes, or platforms. Research institutions may hold a part of the capital share, which potentially generates opportunities for research funding.

Academic institutions, often in cooperation with local government, may also favor the creation of innovative *startup companies*, and may support them through incubators. Typically, an *incubator* offers opportunities and support facilities to creative individuals (for example, PhD students) to try innovative business ideas by starting a new entrepreneurial venture. Experience shows that startups do have high rates of failure, but the minority that have gone on to be successful includes companies that have become large and influential.

Another successful approach to foster innovation is through creation of specific institutions whose mission is to engage in applied research and technology transfer from research to society, and in particular industry. The largest and most successful application-oriented research organization in Europe is the German Fraunhofer-Gesellschaft, consisting of sixty applied research institutes, which cover health, security, communication, energy, and the environment. Funding is 30% by public institutions (federal and local governments) and 70% by contracts with industry and by successful competition in national and international applied research funding programs. Figure 1.5[11] illustrates how application-oriented research institutions are positioned in the research arena. The horizontal axis shows the spectrum of activities from basic research to full commercial exploitation of the derived innovations, while the vertical axis shows the intensity of research activities. The figure shows that academic institutions mainly focus on basic research, while industry focuses mostly on exploitable innovations. Applied research institutions sit somewhat in the middle.

The world of research also interacts directly with the civil society. A demand for research may in fact originate directly from the civil society. Researchers may be involved in initiatives that disseminate research and innovation to the general public. This interaction is increasingly important today, due to the profound impact of research on humans, their daily life, and human relations. To account for this role, the Triple Helix model has been generalized to the *Quadruple Helix* model, as a framework in which not only government, academia, and industry, but also the civil society are seen as key actors promoting a participatory approach to innovation. Through this model, "strategy development and decision-making are exposed to feedback from key stakeholders, resulting in socially accountable policies and practices" [6]. To conclude, today research has constant interaction with the real world. The myth of the ivory tower, where researchers work in isolation from mundane factors and practicalities, on abstruse theories and in secluded laboratories, is far from contemporary reality. Research is deeply rooted into the world's fabric. The real world is the source of the problems investigated by researchers. Their

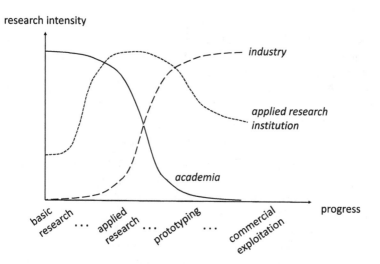

Fig. 1.5 The roles of academia, industry, and applied research institutions

---

[11]This figure has been adapted from a presentation by A. Fuggetta, which describes the mission of Cefriel, an Italian institution with a similar role of Fraunhofer, on a smaller scale.

results are transferred to the world through a range of modalities, spanning from dissemination of new knowledge to societal innovations. The continuous interaction between research and society, which has happened since the scientific revolution in the early seventeenth century, has been accelerating at a very high speed in recent times. The transformation from the pre-industrial to the industrial society took more than one century. The transformation from the industrial society into the digital (or information) society has taken place in a few decades, and is changing the world even more radically.

The need for researchers to engage with society became stronger and stronger. Because often the results of their scientific work can be used to affect the real world, researchers need to engage with society in discussing goals and directions, and setting priorities. On the one hand, researchers have the responsibility to explain the results of science to the general public, to help people understand the effects and limits of research, without distortions. On the other hand, researchers must be ready not only to address the challenges of difficult technical problems, but also by ethical issues raised by the potential use of their research in the world in which we live.

1.6   A Closer Look at Informatics

In this section, I briefly delve into Informatics, the research field that has a privileged role in this book. Compared to other sciences, Informatics is a young discipline. It has developed after World War II with the invention of digital computing technologies. Nevertheless, in half a century it produced spectacular, revolutionary changes in the world, impacting all aspects of human life and society.

Informatics was born with digital computers. This original root is clearly evidenced by the alternative name for the field (*Computer Science*), which is still dominant in North America. The term Informatics is instead dominant in Europe.[12] The term Computer Science was criticized by an eminent researcher, E.W. Dijkstra. A quote often attributed to him says:

> Computer science is no more about computers than astronomy is about telescopes.

From a research standpoint, Informatics is a broad field that comprises a set of sub-areas. The ERC defines the sector as shown in Table 1.5. Informatics has strong interactions with most other scientific fields, and is intrinsically multi-faceted. It has a formal science facet, exemplified by theoretical research that studies formal models of computation, a constructive science facet, which for example investigates new algorithms to solve practical problems, new computational devices, or new user interfaces, and an analytic science facet, exemplified by studies of performance of complex architectures or research observing how programmers work.

---

[12]The ERC takes an ecumenical approach and calls the research sector "Computer Science and Informatics."

Table 1.5 ERC specification for Computer Science and Informatics

Computer Science and Informatics
Computer architecture, pervasive computing, ubiquitous computing
Computer systems, parallel/distributed systems, sensor networks, embedded systems, cyber-physical systems
Software engineering, operating systems, computer languages
Theoretical computer science, formal methods, and quantum computing
Cryptology, security, privacy, quantum cryptography
Algorithms, distributed, parallel and network algorithms, algorithmic game theory
Artificial intelligence, intelligent systems, multi agent systems
Computer graphics, computer vision, multi media, computer games
Human computer interaction and interface, visualisation and natural language processing
Web and information systems, database systems, information retrieval and digital libraries, data fusion
Machine learning, statistical data processing and applications using signal processing (e.g. speech, image, video)
Scientific computing, simulation and modelling tools
Bioinformatics, biocomputing, and DNA and molecular computation

Most important, Informatics has become pervasive and has revolutionized all other sciences. It has migrated into *things* of any kind, giving them the ability to behave autonomously and to communicate with other *things*, creating an *Internet-of-Things* (IoT). The boundary between the physical and the digital world is progressively disappearing. This has changed, for example, how experiments are made in many branches of science. As another example, massive amounts of data, often called *big data*, which were traditionally unavailable and even unconceivable in the past, are now stored in digital form, widely and easily accessible to researchers throughout the world.[13] Powerful algorithms can then be developed to extract useful information from the data and *learn* all kinds of interesting relations among them. This is happening in almost all sectors: from particle Physics to Art, from Astrophysics to Biology and Agriculture. *Data science*—which developed within Informatics—is taking over many domains and the importance of managing and sharing data is being felt throughout the scientific community. Some people push the issue even further and ask whether doing science is becoming indistinguishable from analyzing large data sets algorithmically. It is now common to hear, for example, biologists say that "to be a biologist, nowadays, you need to be a statistician, or even a programmer. You need to be able to work with algorithms."

Radical changes have already occurred in many areas and generated new opportunities for interdisciplinary research in collaboration and au-pair with almost all other research areas. The field of Bioinformatics has become mature and is

---

[13]I discuss here the effect of "big data" on research, although most sectors of society—industry, finance, health, . . . —are also deeply affected.

explicitly mentioned in the ERC classification, but many others are emerging. Other examples include, among others, new energy production and distribution systems (in collaboration with energy engineers), autonomous vehicles (in collaboration with mechanical engineers), or natural language understanding systems (in collaboration with linguists).

Informatics has been characterized by an unprecedented speed of transformation of research results into products and practical innovations. Let us consider as an example the World Wide Web, which is now considered as a commodity in our society. Tim Berners-Lee conceived the idea of the Web at CERN in 1989 and 2 years later (in 1991) published the first web site. In 1993, 130 web sites were created worldwide. They were over 1 million in 1997 and over 1630 billion in 2018.

As another example, Informatics research develops intelligent algorithms that can be trained to learn from large amounts of collected data. Machine learning is now increasingly used in many areas and spectacular success stories have been reported. For example, image recognition applications based on deep learning algorithms are now routinely used for crime and terrorism prevention.

Since the products of Informatics research often have direct consequences on humans, on society, and on the environment, ethical questions arise for the researcher, which cannot be ignored or postponed. More on this crucial topic is discussed in Chap. 6.

1.7 Conclusions

This chapter presented an introduction to scientific research, emphasizing the benefits of looking at the field with an open mindset, recognizing the benefits of a variety of contributions and diversity of approaches in the discovery processes, which must be both creative and systematic. We observed that research both generates new knowledge and leverages new knowledge to change the world. The society in which we live has been largely enabled and shaped by advances in research. Research enabled continuous progress, which could liberate humans from the fatigue of heavy and dangerous work, could defeat diseases that caused premature death, could provide better living conditions and more education.

The picture, however, has its dark side and there are serious concerns about the future. First, the benefits have not been for all. There is still a huge divide between regions of the world and even within the same societies. There are cases where almost all individuals are given equal opportunity to enjoy the benefits of progress, while in many other cases most individuals are deprived. Second, the progress that started with the industrial revolution and continued until now has affected the planet in which we live. The impact on the environment of the current development model has reached an alarming stage and is becoming incompatible with the future of human life on our planet. The digital society into which we are moving generates further serious concerns; it is challenging the notions of living individuals and society, as they developed in the history of mankind. The speed at which this is happening requires researchers to rethink their role and the priorities of their work. They also need to face the inescapable ethical questions due to the impact of research in the real world. These questions need to be addressed as part of their research.

1.8 Further Reading

The reader can refer to the thrilling book "Sapiens—A Brief History of Human Kind" by Harari [19] for a grand historical perspective, and in particular to the illuminating chapter on "The scientific revolution", which has been widely cited here. Harari's subsequent book "Homo Deus—A Brief History of Tomorrow" [20] is a thought-provoking sequel, which looks into the future, to understand where humankind is heading.

The book "Pasteur's Quadrant" by D.E. Stokes [54] presents an excellent discussion of research and its application. It reflects on and criticizes Bush's dichotomy between basic and applied science and argues for interactive roles of science and technology.

Chapter 2
Research Methodology

This chapter focuses on research methodology. Literally, methodology means the *study of methods*. Methods are actionable rational principles that can guide humans in accomplishing tasks. Research methods provide guidance to achieve scientific results. The discussion starts in Sect. 2.1 with a brief history of the human understanding of science as it developed over centuries. It was not until the work of, among others, Francis Bacon, Galileo Galilei, and Isaac Newton—from the early seventeenth till the early eighteenth century—that the need for methods to guide scientists through discoveries was explicitly realized. As I presented in Sect. 1.3, this sparked the scientific revolution that gave birth to the modern society. Discussions on methods continued to our age and will continue in the future, through the contributions of scientists and philosophers.

The scientific method developed during the scientific revolution is the *experimental method*, introduced in Sect. 2.2. Through the experimental method, scientists critically observe the physical world and try to discover laws that describe its behavior and predict future manifestations. Section 2.3 discusses and formalizes the process followed by researchers in the discovery process. It presents the two primitive logic mechanisms used by scientists in the process: deduction and induction. By using mathematical logic, it is possible to explain the intrinsic differences in the two logic mechanisms, which leads to the fundamental distinction between demonstrable proofs and disprovable conjectures, which are at the heart of the experimental method.

Section 2.4 discusses the limits of discoveries, which lead to questioning the notion of *truth* of scientific results. The solutions to research problems are often only approximate solutions that work within well-defined contexts and are accepted until better solutions are found. By and large, agreement on validity of research results is a complex social process.

The experimental method is the reference method used in analytic research. Through experiments, researchers assess validity of their results. Research validation through different kinds of experiments also applies to other kinds of research, such constructive research, and partly even formal research. Validation

© Springer Nature Switzerland AG 2020
C. Ghezzi, *Being a Researcher*, https://doi.org/10.1007/978-3-030-45157-8_2

is an essential component of any research method. Validation assesses a given result, compares a result against others, and shows how a result may be improved. Final reflections on validation are provided in Sect. 2.5, especially referring to Informatics.

2.1 A Historical Perspective

The aspiration to understand the world and be able to explain and predict world phenomena is connatural to human beings. Starting from Greek philosophers—like Plato and Aristotle—philosophers for centuries reflected on how humans can develop an understanding of the world. We defined science as a systematically organized body of knowledge. How is such body of knowledge built? What method do scientists follow? For centuries what mankind called science mostly referred to beliefs that had no scientific justification, but instead came from religion, superstition, or unsupported statements. Most of them were later found by science to be wrong. A well-known example of a wrong belief is the Aristotelian and Ptolemaic view of the universe, which placed the Earth at its center [30]. The notion of a scientific method, as we understand it today, was born in the seventeenth century during the scientific revolution. In particular, the work by Francis Bacon, Galileo Galilei, and Isaac Newton developed the foundations of what we know today as the *experimental method*. The method is at the heart of the analytic research style, which observes and tries to understand unknown (natural and physical) phenomena. The experimental method prescribes that research results must be supported by evidence-based argumentations, which rely on careful experiments and observations of the phenomenon under study. Hereafter I briefly describe their main contributions to the development of modern science.

Francis Bacon wrote the book *Novum Organum* (or *New Method*) in 1620, in which he argues that humans cannot just passively observe the nature to understand it. They cannot rely on luck of observations, but need to be proactive and perform *experiments*. Experiments are actions, leading to observations, performed with the explicit goal of confirming or refuting a hypothesis that is meant to be an explanation of a given natural phenomenon.

Francis Bacon's idea fully matured, both in theory and in practice, in the foundational work of Galileo Galilei. Galileo was a physicist, an astronomer, an engineer, and a philosopher. He developed a systematic approach to research, which is based on observing, collecting, and carefully analyzing data about the phenomenon under study. Once a theory is formulated to explain the phenomenon, it must be challenged by experiments, which may disprove or confirm the theory. Because of his contribution to devising a systematic and rigorous method to guide research, Galileo has been considered by Albert Einstein as the father of the modern science.

The essence of Galileo's method is traditionally explained by referring to the Pisa leaning tower experiment,[1] where he is said to have dropped two spheres of different masses from the top of the tower to disprove what people believed at the time: that heavy objects fall faster than lighter ones, in direct proportion to their weight. This belief was in accordance with Aristotle's theory of gravity, assumed to be valid at the time, which stated that objects fall at speed proportional to their mass. Galileo instead argued that that bodies of the same material falling through the same medium would fall at the same speed, regardless of their mass. This led to Galileo's *law of free fall*, which states that, in the absence of air resistance (i.e., in vacuum), all bodies fall with the same acceleration, independent of their mass.

Galileo is perhaps the first example of a scientist who is aware of his intellectual responsibility for integrity. He taught us that a scientist should not try to use the data with the goal of getting evidence that would confirm previous knowledge, or would conform to dominant orthodoxy or ideology. Rational argumentations must be used to arrive at whatever conclusions a careful analysis of evidence would suggest, even if they are not conformant with current beliefs. He was indeed a man of high integrity. He did not hesitate to contradict the doctrine of the Catholic Church, which at the time followed the Ptolemaic view that the earth was at the center of the solar system. Galileo had to appear before the Roman Inquisition and was eventually accused of heresy. He was forced to recant his views, and was sentenced to house arrest for the rest of his life.

Galileo also taught us that scientists must engage themselves in what today we call reach-out activities. He did not just speak to his peer scientists, but brought his revolutionary theories to the entire society. He realized that scientists must disseminate the results of research to the general public, especially when they have a profound impact on society. This must be done using a rigorous but understandable language. In a book titled "Dialog Concerning the Two Chief World Systems" he presented a discussion involving three men. One (named Salviati) advocates the scientific method, and presents Galileo's views of astronomy. Another (named Sagredo) takes a neutral position. A third (named Simplicio) holds firm on the geocentric—Ptolemaic—view of the cosmos. Although Galileo did not explicitly conclude that Salviati is right (and Simplicio is wrong), all the arguments that refute geocentrism clearly emerge from his book. More details on Galileo's long confrontation with the prevalent views of science at his time can be found in Box 2.1.

Another fundamental contribution of Galileo's work is the equal importance of theory and application in research. He used tools and built his own to support his research, like his famous telescope used to observe the geography of the Moon, the phases of Venus, and the moons of Jupiter.[2] In building his telescope, he was among the first to use the refracting principle to observe the stars. He also devised

---

[1] There is no real evidence that the experiment actually took place. Most historians consider it to be an explanatory example rather than a physical experiment.

[2] Interestingly, Galileo built the telescope and used it even before he had a theory to explain how it worked. He developed the theory afterwards, to justify his observations. This is another striking example of the possible interplay between theory and practice in research.

and improved a geometric and military compass suitable for use by gunners and surveyors, developed a new and safer way of elevating cannons accurately, and a way of quickly computing the charge of gunpowder for cannonballs of different sizes and materials. Finally, he devised engineering schemes to alleviate river flooding. In modern jargon, Galileo Galilei was both a scientist and a visionary innovator. His research contributions spanned from basic science to technology and applications. He was both a physicist and an engineer.

Yet another fundamental contribution by Galileo was his recognition of the fundamental role of mathematics in scientific research. This was clearly formulated in 1623 in an essay titled *Il Saggiatore (The Assayer)*. Let me quote his beautiful words[3]

> the universe ... cannot be understood unless one first learns to comprehend the language and read the letters in which it is composed. It is written in the language of mathematics, and its characters are triangles, circles, and other geometric figures without which it is humanly impossible to understand a single word of it; without these, one wanders about in a dark labyrinth.

Isaac Newton brought to completion the intellectual revolution started by Galileo Galilei, through his fundamental contributions to science and to the development of a scientific method based on mathematics. He was born the year Galileo died. Some people consider his book "The Mathematical Principles of Natural Philosophy", written in 1687, as the most important book in modern science history. It paved the road for the extensive and fundamental use of mathematics in research, which is now an unquestioned principle. In Netwton's work, Galileo's intuition that mathematics is the language of science was brought to its full glory: through mathematics, physical phenomena can be modeled in a rigorous and abstract way. The mathematical model justifies the possible observations and predicts future behaviors. Isaac Newton is famous for his theory of motion, which explains and predicts the movement of all bodies in the universe, through the three well-known mathematical laws of mechanics, described in Box 2.2.

2.2   Lessons Learnt from History

The previous section presented some fundamental contributions from the scientific revolution in the seventeenth century, which laid the foundations of the modern view of scientific research. In particular, they shaped our understanding of how scientific

---

[3] A similar statement was expressed in modern time by the famous physicist Richard Feynman [15]. These are his equally beautiful words:

> To those who do not know mathematics it is difficult to get across a real feeling as to the beauty, the deepest beauty, of nature ... If you want to learn about nature, to appreciate nature, it is necessary to understand the language that she speaks in.

Box 2.1: Galileo Galilei's Heresy

Galileo's studies of observational astronomy led him to champion heliocentrism against Ptolemaic geocentrism, which was officially adopted by the Catholic doctrine at the time. The matter was investigated by the Roman Inquisition in 1615, under a request of the Pope to "summon Galileo and warn him to abandon his opinions and, in case of refusal, oblige him to reject the theory and forbid teaching, defending, and studying it." The Inquisition concluded that heliocentrism was "foolish and absurd in philosophy, and formally heretical since it explicitly contradicts in many places the sense of Holy Scripture." Galileo later defended his views in his book titled "Dialogue Concerning the Two Chief World Systems." His position, however, appeared to attack the Pope. He was tried again by the Inquisition in 1633. The Inquisition found him suspect of heresy and forced him to recant. While under house arrest, he wrote (and published in The Netherlands) a book "Two New Sciences", in which he summarized and systematized the work he had done earlier in his life. The book is organized as a dialogue that takes place in 4 days and involves the same main characters of the "Dialog Concerning the Two Chief World Systems" (Sagredo, Salviati, and Simplicio). The book covers materials and motion, setting the rules of kinematics.

Galileo plays a fundamental role in the history of science not only for his seminal contributions, but also for his forceful and passionate statements about freedom of research from religion and politics. He became the emblem of the conflict between dogmatism and scientific evidence. A popular legend attributes to him the words "and yet it moves", which he said after recanting his theory that the Earth rotates around the Sun.

In a famous play written after World War II, German dramatist Bertolt Brecht depicts the conflict between dogmatism and science very vividly, but also questions the values of integrity and constancy in the face of oppression. At the end of the play, he depicts old Galileo, living in his house under arrest, with a priest controlling his activities. Galileo is visited by one of his former students, Andrea. Galileo gives him a copy of "Two New Sciences" and asks him to smuggle it out of Italy for dissemination. Andrea now understands that Galileo's actions were heroic and that he recanted to be able to continue his research. However, Galileo insists that he did that to avoid torture.

---

theories are discovered, formulated, and validated through the *experimental method*. According to it, the research process roughly proceeds in the following way. The researcher who studies a natural or physical phenomenon formulates a theory that tries to explain it. The theory is in agreement with previous observations of the

> **Box 2.2: Newton's Laws of Mechanics**
>
> Newton's laws of mechanics are perhaps the earliest example of a mathematical description of physical phenomena, which became part of our common knowledge. Newton's first law says: "Every body continues in its state of rest, or of uniform motion in a right line, unless it is compelled to change that state by forces impressed upon it." Formally,
>
> $$\Delta \mathbf{v} = 0 \iff \sum_i \mathbf{F}_i = 0 \qquad (2.1)$$
>
> where $\Delta \mathbf{v}$ is the body's change of speed and $\mathbf{F}_i$ are the forces applied to it. Newton's second law correlates a body's acceleration to the force applied to it:
>
> $$\mathbf{F} = m\mathbf{a} \qquad (2.2)$$
>
> where $\mathbf{F}$ is the force on the body's mass m, and $\mathbf{a}$ is its acceleration.
>
> Newton's third law states that "for every action, there is an equal and opposite reaction." That is, whenever object A pushes on object B with force $\mathbf{F}_A$, object B pushes object A with force $\mathbf{F}_B$, where
>
> $$\mathbf{F}_B = -\mathbf{F}_A \qquad (2.3)$$

phenomenon. This step is largely driven by creativity and ingenuity.[4] The theory is then challenged by experiments, and possibly refined or modified iteratively. Let us look more deeply into the experimental method. Observations of the phenomenon under study lead the scientist to conjecture possible explanations, which are consolidated as a set of *hypotheses*. These are refined into a formal *theory*, typically expressed in mathematical terms. This step is an *induction*. Induction is a reasoning method in which the premises—the observations—supply evidence for the validity of the conclusions—the hypotheses. It is the essence of the creative step that leads to scientific discoveries. Many factors drive this creative step: intuition, experience, analogy, analytical skills, mathematical skills, and so on. Two main specific reasoning mechanisms play a fundamental role: abstraction and generalization.

Abstraction is the act of deliberately ignoring certain details and focusing on the essence of a phenomenon. It is also the act through which a real phenomenon—e.g., occurring in the physical world—is denoted, i.e., represented using a language or a

---

[4]Hereafter, I use the terms creativity and ingenuity interchangeably.

notation.[5] For example, in the Pisa leaning tower experiment by Galileo, abstraction leads to the decision of ignoring irrelevant details, like color of the falling body. The precise description of the phenomenon, in this case the use of formal terms like "body" or "acceleration", is also an abstraction. Reference to the ideal condition of "free fall in a vacuum" is a further abstraction.

Generalization draws a conclusion for a population from premises about individuals. In the example, it generalizes the same value of acceleration to *all* falling bodies.

The tentative theory that is conjectured as a possible explanation of the phenomenon cannot be accepted based on pure faith, but must be challenged by further experiments to validate it. A theory may in fact turn out to be inaccurate, or even totally wrong. Validation is done through *experiments*. The step that derives new experiments from hypotheses is a *deduction* made from the theory. In this decisive step, a scientist predicts facts that must be observable if the hypotheses holds. Through carefully designed experiments, which lead to new observations, the scientist may then either show the fallacy of the theory or may find a confirmation of the hypotheses. Confirmation increases confidence in the conjectured theory. A failure instead indicates that the hypotheses does not capture the phenomenon under study. Hypotheses must be refined or modified, or new hypotheses must be formulated, and then the validation cycle is repeated until the scientist can formulate a satisfactory theory that explains the phenomenon. The process described here in words is succinctly described by the iterative loop shown in Fig. 2.1.

As an example, let us refer to Newton's laws of motion. They were never contradicted by any experiments in everyday life.[6] Thus they are assumed to be true and can be used to predict the motion of physical bodies in most practical conditions. Another example are the laws of thermodynamics, which explain how energy can be exchanged between physical systems. Yet another example is Ohm's law, which states that the current through a conductor between two points is directly proportional to the voltage across the two points.

In the first half of the twentieth century, the revolutionary theories developed in particular by physicists (like Albert Einstein, Max Planck, Niels Bohr, and many others) opened heated and foundational debates on the very notions of science and of scientific truth, which involved scientists and philosophers. It gave impetus to the development of philosophy of science. The continuous evolution of science has fueled the debate, which continues today with new arguments. History of the scientific thought and philosophy of science are fascinating subjects. A discussion of these issues would take us on a path that goes beyond the scope of this book. For additional remarks and some pointers to the literature, the reader may refer to Boxes 2.3, 2.4, 2.5.

---

[5]To understand more the notion of abstraction, the reader may refer to the work by Jeff Kramer [28], who cogently articulates how this skill is key to Informatics.

[6]They are valid with respect to inertial frames of reference, which hold in most practical settings. In particular, the speed one works with must be much less than the speed of light, otherwise relativistic mechanics must be used instead of Newton's mechanics.

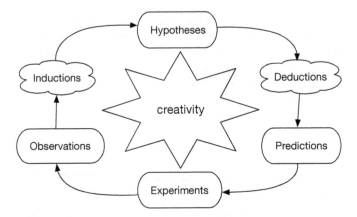

Fig. 2.1 The experimental method

Box 2.3: Philosophy of Science

The modern philosophy of science was born after World War I in Vienna. A group of eminent philosophers, scientists, and mathematicians grouped together in a permanent seminar from 1924 until 1936, called *Wiener Kreis* (*Vienna Circle*). The members of the seminar, inspired by the recent revolutionary developments of science, such as Albert Einstein's general relativity and David Hilbert's axiomatization of geometry, aimed at founding philosophy on a scientific view of the world, keeping it separate from metaphysics. The philosopher Moritz Schlick chaired the group, which included—among others—philosopher and logician Rudolf Carnap, mathematician Hans Hahn, sociologist and philosopher Otto Neurath. Mathematician Kurt Gödel—Hans Hahn's doctoral student—was an occasional guest, while Karl Popper and Ludwig Wittgenstein did not participate, but interacted with the group. The Vienna Circle dissolved in 1936, when Moritz Schlick died, and a diaspora of its members was caused by anti-semitism in Austria. Karl Sigmund's book, titled "Exact Thinking in Demented Times: The Vienna Circle and the Epic Quest for the Foundations of Science" [52], is a fascinating read about this exciting historical period.

Karl Popper and Thomas Kuhn are two well-known philosophers who gave foundational contributions to philosophy of science, starting from the fertile grounds founded by the Vienna Circle. Their work had a profound influence on the modern view of science (see Boxes 2.4, 2.5).

Let us go back to our discussion about lessons learnt. Falsification of a theory by further experiments is not necessarily a failure that leads research to a dead end. The failure often produces a fertile ground for further progress of knowledge and generation of new findings, which then survive subsequent experiments. The

---

Box 2.4: Karl Popper: The Falsifiability Principle

Karl Popper is known for his book on the development of scientific theories [43] (first published in 1934), which introduces the fundamental notion of *falsifiability*. Popper argues that scientific theories are universal propositions that are conjectural and hypothetical in nature, and can only be validated indirectly by reference to their consequences. Popper starts from the observation that no number of positive outcomes at the level of experimental testing can confirm a scientific theory, but a single counterexample is logically decisive to dismiss it. This demonstrates the superior role of falsification as opposed to positive verification. Popper goes on and defines falsifiability of a proposition T as follows:

> if T is false, then (in principle), T can be shown to be false, by observation or by experiment

Popper elected falsifiability as the criterion of demarcation between what is and what is not genuinely scientific: a theory should be considered scientific if, and only if, it is falsifiable.

Box 2.5: Thomas Kuhn: Normal Science and Paradigm Shifts

Thomas Kuhn developed a new theory of science in his influential book "The Structure of Scientific Revolutions" [31]. He argues that science does not progress via a linear accumulation of new knowledge, but undergoes periodic revolutions. Most of the time, science (what he calls *normal science*) operates within a set of given assumptions and a body of knowledge—a *paradigm*—that are taken as given and not subject to testing. Normal science is the process of elaboration of the paradigm in ever more detail. At some stage, a revolutionary change occurs, which leads to a *paradigm shift*. The revolutionary change is driven by the inability to explain some elements within the current paradigm. For example, Newton's theory of motion cannot explain the perihelion[7] precession[8] of Mercury's orbit. A paradigm shift—Einstein's general relativity theory—explains this phenomenon. Kuhn provides the following examples of paradigm shifts in optics. In the eighteenth century, Newtonian optics was the dominant paradigm, which considered light as consisting of physical particles. In the nineteenth century, a paradigm shift led to viewing light as optical waves. In the twentieth century, Albert Einstein and Max Planck developed the dual wave-like and particle-like nature of light as consisting of photons, which led to another paradigm shift. Kuhn's notion that science progresses through phases of normal science and paradigm shifts that generate a revolutionary discontinuity in its progress became widely accepted.

invention of the electric battery by Alessandro Volta, described in Box 2.6, provides a good example of this lucky, but not unusual case.

Our discussion shows that a theory derived from observations becomes accepted as long as observations deriving by carefully designed experiments confirm it. An experiment leading to data that confirm a hypothesis do not prove it, but it may increase confidence in its validity. This can be summarized in Einstein's words as:

No amount of experimentation can ever prove me right; a single experiment can prove me wrong.

Drawing an analogy to Informatics, this is exactly the same as when we test a program on given data and the output results are the ones we expect. The only conclusion we can draw is that the results are *consistent* with the hypothesis under experimental evaluation, not that they *prove* correctness of the program.

This is eloquently expressed by this is famous statement by Turing laureate E.W. Dijkstra:

Program testing can be used to show the presence of bugs, but never to show their absence.

To summarize, the experimental method is based on three cornerstones:

• Centrality of *observations* and *experiments* to understand the phenomena under study. No previous bias or belief should limit the scientist in her observations and experiments.

Box 2.6: Invention of the Electric Battery

In the late 1700s, Luigi Galvani—an anatomy professor in Bologna—while making experiments on dead frogs, noticed that muscular contraction could be obtained by applying a bi-metallic arc connecting the lumbar nerves and the thigh muscle. He hypothesized the existence of animal electricity accumulated ion the frog. Alessandro Volta, who was working at the Royal School in Como, applauded the discovery, but decided to investigate it further himself. Repeated experiments and rigorous measures convinced him that Galvani's theory was wrong. The electrical flow was not generated by animal electricity accumulated in the frog, but by the contact between two metals. Eventually, this observation led Volta to his most famous invention: the electric battery. Designed in 1799, it was made of alternating copper and zinc conductive discs with a weakly acidic layer separating each pair of metals. The contact between the metals produced electricity in the form of sparks.

---

[7] The perihelion is the point in the orbit that is nearest to the sun.

[8] The precession is a change in the orientation of the rotational axis.

- Through *ingenuity*, observations lead to hypotheses, which explain the phenomena. Hypotheses are formalized as a conjectured *theory* through *mathematics*.
- Experiments are generated to justify the theory. Experiments may either invalidate or confirm the predictions made by the theory. A theory can only stand on rational justifications, not on myths or faith.

As we discussed in Chap. 1, the scientific revolution in the seventeenth century generated the industrial revolution, which led to our contemporary society. It also shaped the way we conceive science and research today. The work by Galileo not only laid the foundations of the experimental method, through which the scientific results in natural and physical sciences can be validated. From his work we can also draw two further lessons that are especially valid today:

- There is no dichotomy between science and technology, or pure science and applied science. They are both equally valuable. A scientist may successfully engage in both, and they can even coexist in the same scientist. Galileo demonstrated that novel applications of science can solve societal problems and lead to societal changes. Applications, in turn, can be the fuel of new fundamental research.
- Scientists do not live in a bubble. Researchers have a social responsibility. They must engage with society and they must do it according to ethical principles. This is the lesson learnt from Galileo's strenuous defense for freedom of research.

2.3 Inductive and Deductive Reasoning

The iterative process in Fig. 2.1 summarizes the experimental method as an iterative process. The process is not a mechanical workflow, but is driven by ingenuity and controlled by rigor. A rigorous approach is needed both to turn observations of real-world phenomena into possible explanatory hypotheses, to formalize them in a theory, and to deduce predictions, which lead to further observations, with the goal of progressively validating the theory. As I mentioned, two fundamental kinds of reasoning mechanisms take place in this iterative process: induction and deduction. They are the concepts we dissect in this section. Both induction and deduction can be formalized using mathematical logic. The formalization helps understand them better and sheds more light on the iterative process illustrated by Fig. 2.1. *Deduction* is a process of reasoning from one or more statements—premises—to reach a logically certain conclusion: it infers the conclusion from the premises. This is also called a *syllogism*: we arrive at a conclusion based on propositions that are asserted and assumed to be true. In deductive inferences, what is inferred is *necessarily true* if the premises from which the conclusion is inferred are true. That is, the truth of the premises guarantees the truth of the conclusion: it is a *proof*.

In the context of the iterative process in Fig. 2.1, deduction is applied to make predictions based on current hypotheses. Predicted truths are then used to validate hypotheses through experiments, which may confirm or disprove them.

Let us examine a typical deductive inference rule, called *modus ponens*. The rule can be described as follows:

From the truth of the statement *P implies Q* (called *major premise*) and the truth of statement *P* (called *minor premise*, or *antecedent*) we deduce *Q* (called *consequent*, or *prediction*).

Formally, this can be expressed in mathematical logic by the following formula:

$$[((P{\rightarrow}Q){\wedge}P) \vdash Q]$$

where $\rightarrow$ stands for implication, $\wedge$ stands for "and", and $\vdash$ stands for "logical consequence" (or "entailment").

A classical example of modus ponens is the following:

"All men are mortal", "Socrates is a man", from which we deduce "Socrates is mortal."

where "All men are mortal" is the major premise, "Socrates is a man" is the minor premise, and "Socrates is mortal" is the consequence.

Another example of modus ponens is:

"All Italians like pasta", "Alessandro is Italian", from which we deduce that "Alessandro likes pasta"

In this example, deduction works as follows. We start from an assumed truth "All Italians like pasta", which is a formal statement of a theory that captures the culinary preferences of a population. Given the observation that an individual is a member of the population, we deduce the individual's culinary preference.

I now use variations of the example to discuss *induction*. Suppose that we do not have a theory, like "All Italians like pasta." Suppose, instead, that we repeatedly observe Italian individuals, and that all of them like pasta. Observations lead us to postulate the following generalizing hypothesis:

All Italians like pasta.

We already observed that *generalization* is an inductive inference. It is a creative action that infers commonalities from observations. Differently from deductive inference, which leads to necessary conclusions, inductive inference leads to non-necessary conclusions. In fact, although from *P implies Q* and *P* we can derive the truth of *Q*, knowing that *Q* is true, we cannot derive *P implies Q* and *P*. Entailment is not symmetric. Specifically, the generalization that "All Italians like pasta" cannot be assumed to hold by repeatedly observing individuals who are Italian and who like pasta. We may eventually run into an Italian who does not like pasta. Likewise, having observed that Camilla likes pasta we cannot derive that Camilla is Italian, even assuming that we know that "All Italians like pasta" (for example, Camilla might be Spanish and she might like pasta).

This brings us to understand the limitations of inductive reasoning. Induction is the logical process that leads to *non-necessary conclusions*, as opposed to deduction, where conclusions are certain. Because conclusions are not certain, we need to provide strong support for them, through a reasoning process that combines rigor and ingenuity, since we cannot aim at *proving* their validity. We need to challenge the inferred hypotheses through experiments and further observations. In the example, we would need to conduct more experiments with additional, carefully chosen individuals of Italian nationality to check whether the observations confirm that they like pasta. Experiments are expected to comply with the predictions made by modus ponens. That is, given the tentative theory $\forall X[(Italian(X) \rightarrow LikesPasta(X)]$, modus ponens predicts the observation $LikesPasta$(Federico) for an experiment made with an individual—Federico—satisfying the constraint $Italian$(Federico).

In designing such experiments, we should do our best to select individuals who are likely to challenge the postulated hypothesis. For example, we should try with individuals from different Italian regions, to make sure that the hypothesis equally applies across all of them. We may also try with people of different age groups, different social groups, etc. In other terms, deductive reasoning should not be applied blindly to make predictions, but should aim at challenging the hypothesis and possibly falsify it through experiments.

We have seen generalization as a typical and very important type of reasoning that leads to a non-necessary conclusion, which is drawn from a number of cases of which something is true, inferring that the same thing is true for the whole class. Generalization is supported by a large number of unbiased observations in a given data set (in the example, individuals of Italian nationality) that do not violate the inferred property. Support increases with the size of the data set and with diversity of the data within the chosen data set.

Philosopher C. S. Peirce (see Box 2.7) distinguished between *induction*, the term he uses to refer to generalization, and *abduction*. Abduction denotes a kind of inferential reasoning that we might informally call *explanation*. In our running example, assuming that all Italians like pasta (the major premise) and observing that an individual likes pasta (the consequence), one may *explain* the observation by postulating that the individual is Italian. In this case, the data set would need to include individuals of different nationalities. The explanation is plausible if no observed individual of non Italian nationality likes pasta while all Italians like it. Formally, abduction infers P from $((P \rightarrow Q) \wedge Q)$.

Inferential reasoning was also studied extensively by philosopher and mathematician Bertrand Russell. He especially discussed the role and pitfalls of induction (see Box 2.8).

To summarize, in analytic research the notion of a non-necessary inference is at the heart of scientific discoveries. It is no surprise that philosophers of science actively investigated this notion, especially in the context of natural and physical sciences.

Let us now go back to the simple case of research on culinary preferences we have been using as a running example. It is unlikely that research results might be expressed in absolute terms by a theory like "All Italians like pasta." Surely, there are also Italians who don't like pasta, and for example instead prefer risotto as a first course. To account for that, one might summarize the findings through a *qualitative theory*: "most Italians like pasta." To be more precise, however, one should try to express the findings through a *quantitative theory*. To account for uncertainty, which

Box 2.7: Charles S. Peirce: Induction vs. Abduction

Charles S. Peirce (1834–1914) [42] gave contributions that shed new light on the process of scientific inquiry and its relevance to everyday thinking. He thoroughly investigated the limits of inferential reasoning in deriving knowledge. Hereafter I use Peirce's terminology, which distinguishes between three kinds of inference: deduction, induction, and abduction. These are briefly explained here using Peirce's own terminology. Peirce focused on arguments that contain the following elements: a *Case*, a *Result*, and a *Rule*, where

1. *Case* is the antecedent in the argument that describes a fact;
2. *Result* is the observed or experienced consequent;
3. *Rule* is the general principle (the theory) that explains a phenomenon.

Peirce used the example of a bag of white beans to explain the different kinds of inference. To explain deduction (necessary inference) he gives the following example:

> All the beans in the bag are white (Rule)
> These beans are from the bag (Case)
> Therefore these beans must be white (Result)

Deduction describes a reasoning process that tries to answer the following question: Why are the beans we observe white?
Should one observe instead as a result a non-white bean, one would conclude that either the rule or the case do not hold, since in deduction results are always true, as long as premises (rule and case) are true.
Peirce explains induction through the following example:

> These beans are from the bag (Case)
> These beans are white (Result)
> Therefore all the beans in the bag are white (Rule)

Induction describes a reasoning process that tries to answer the following question: What color are all the beans in bag?
Finally, Peirce explains abduction through the following example:

> These beans are white (Result)
> All the beans in the bag are white (Rule)
> Therefore these beans are from the bag (Case)

Abduction describes a reasoning process that tries to answer the following question: Where are these white beans from?

is intrinsic in these kinds of problems, the results might be expressed in terms of probabilities. For example, the research might lead to the following conclusion: "The probability that Italians like pasta is at least 0.8." This means that repeated unbiased experiments performed by research show that if we take random sets of Italians, at least 8 out of 10 like pasta.

This example highlights a very important point. So far we have seen cases of scientific theories expressed as universal laws. This is the case of Galileo's law of free fall, or Newton's laws of mechanics. Often, however, hypotheses are formulated with a degree of uncertainty. For example, medical research has postulated, and confirmed through experimental evidence, a correlation between smoking cigarettes and insurgence of lung cancer. The theory in this case is not expressed in absolute terms (like "smoking cigarettes causes lung cancer"), but as a recurring correlation between two observations. As another example, in the field of software applications, lack of careful requirements analysis prior to development has been shown to lead to "likely" increased development costs and late delivery. To add precision to these theories, which are qualitative in nature, they can be made quantitative by using probabilities. In the medical example, the theory might be formulated by saying that on the average eight out of ten patients with lung cancer are also cigarette smokers.

Hypotheses are also often formulated in a negative way. As an example from medical research, let us consider a study whose goal is to understand whether the measles-mump rubella vaccine causes autism. The hypothesis is framed in a negative form, known in statistics as a *null hypothesis*: the vaccine does not cause autism. Through repeated experiments, researchers try to falsify the null hypothesis, meaning that autism following vaccination occurs at a greater level than expected

---

Box 2.8: Russell's Inductivist Turkey

Non-necessary inferences intrinsically need to be validated by careful experiments. Deductive reasoning is used to generate experiments, which are then performed and observed to either confirm or invalidate the hypotheses conjectured through inductive reasoning. If they do not hold, they need to be revised in the form of new hypotheses. To reinforce the intrinsic limitations of non-necessary inferences, the logician and philosopher Bertrand Russell provided the following vivid image in his book "The Problems of Philosophy" [48]:

> Domestic animals expect food when they see the person who usually feeds them. We know that all these rather crude expectations of uniformity are liable to be misleading. The man who has fed the chicken every day throughout its life at last wrings its neck instead, showing that more refined views as to the uniformity of nature would have been useful to the chicken.

This became popularized as the Bertrand Russel's *inductivist turkey*, where the chicken becomes a turkey and the fatal day when the man wrings its neck is a day before Christmas or Thanksgiving.

by chance alone. Experiments may instead confirm the null hypothesis (as actually happens), meaning that autism following vaccination occurs at a level expected by chance alone. In other terms, there are no grounds for believing that there is a statistical correlation between the two phenomena.

2.4 The Limits of Discoveries

We observed that the results of scientific discoveries are seldom expressed in absolute terms. Absolute truths may be the result of a purely theoretical research which may consist of proving a theorem in a given mathematical setting. Even in mathematics, however, proofs are often the results of a social process and not the result of a one-shot proof by the inventor. As observed in [7], often "it is a social process that determines whether mathematicians feel confident about a theorem." In practice, as shown in Fig. 2.1, research is an iterative process, through which we validate and refine the research results, until they reach an acceptable degree of support from experiments. At each stage of this iterative process, research results are a kind of approximation of the "real" results. In this section I provide a conceptual framework that allows us to speak precisely about "approximation" and in some cases even assess and control it in the research process. We can frame the problem in a logical setting, through the notions of *soundness* and *completeness*. When a researcher studies an unknown phenomenon, he or she[9] comes out with hypotheses, which constitute a theory that tries to explain the phenomenon. The theory is sound if all the potential predictions made by the theory are actually observable for the real phenomenon. In logic terms, a *sound theory* only allows truths to be deduced, but not necessarily all truths. A theory is complete if it can predict all actually observable manifestations. In logic terms, a *complete theory* allows all truths to be deduced, but also possibly non-true facts. Ideally, theories should be both sound and complete. The deducible truths from a theory that are not real truths are called *false positives*. The real truths that are not deducible from a theory are called *false negatives*. Of course deducible truths that are real truths are true positives. The number of false positives and false negatives can be considered as an indication the degree of approximation of the theory. Figure 2.2 provides a graphical representation of sound and complete theories.

For example, let us consider a variation of the toy study on culinary habits I introduced earlier in Sect. 2.3. Suppose that in our study we observe individuals and, based on observations, we wish to build a theory which explains who are the Italians who like pasta. The theory "All Italians like pasta" is complete, since it can predict all Italians who actually like pasta, but it is obviously unsound. For example, it can deduce that even a newborn Italian infant likes pasta. In this example, infants

---

[9]From now on, to avoid gender biased expressions, I alternate between using "he" and "she", to avoid the awkward use of "he or she."

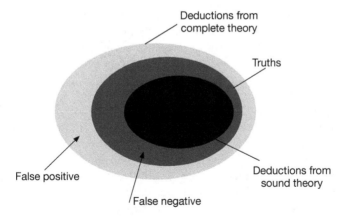

Fig. 2.2 Sound and complete theories, false positives and false negatives. The grey set indicates the set of truths; the dark grey set indicates the set of deductions from a sound theory; the light grey set indicates the set of deductions from a complete theory. Elements in the intersection between the light grey set and the grey set are false positives. Elements in the intersection between the grey set and the dark grey set are false negatives

constitute false positives. A refinement of the theory like "All Italians more than 18 years old like pasta" is also unsound, since some existing adult Italians (who are also false positives) may dislike pasta. The theory "All Italians who ordered pasta more than once in a restaurant last year like pasta"[10] is instead likely to be sound: it describes Italians who can be said to like pasta, but there are certainly more who also like pasta, but either don't go to restaurants or order something else when they go.

Unfortunately, the definitions of sound and complete theory have a purely theoretical nature, and do not lead to practical usage in most real cases. For example, consider the case of an analytical research, which studies a given natural phenomenon. Although through experiments we can observe manifestations of the phenomenon and check whether they are in conformity with the theory (if not, they are false negatives), it may be hard or impossible to check if a manifestation predicted by the theory is actually not possible.

Let us consider the case of constructive research, where the objective is to solve a novel problem, or to find a better solution to an existing problem for which a solution is already known. A typical example in Informatics might be the invention of a clever algorithm to solve a new problem, or a new algorithm that improves significantly the efficiency of existing algorithms, in terms of computation time or consumed storage. The concepts of soundness and completeness equally apply to problem solutions, and algorithms in particular. Moreover, it is possible to quantify the degree of approximation of a given solution. A *sound algorithm* never includes wrong answers, but it might miss a few right answers. A *complete algorithm* never

---

[10] Assuming that one repeats the same order only if satisfied by it.

misses right answers: it provides the complete set of right answers, but it might include a few wrong answers. A sound algorithm is conservative (pessimistic). Its dogma is to remain on safe grounds to get assurance on its results. On the opposite, a complete algorithm is liberal and optimistic. In an attempt to include all results, it delivers more results than may turn out to be invalid. These concepts are intuitively illustrated in Fig. 2.3, which provides an intuitive graphical representation of the results computed by a sound (respectively, complete) algorithm. A *false negative* is a right answer that is not recognized as such by the algorithm. Likewise, a *false positive* is an answer provided by the algorithm that turns out to be wrong. An algorithm is both sound and complete if it provides all and only right answers.

We must acknowledge that in many practical cases it may be impossible or impractical to find a sound and complete algorithm that solves a given problem. We need to accept, and we may be perfectly happy with, approximate solutions. An algorithm may even be neither complete nor sound, and thus it exhibits both false positives and false negative, but it may still be useful in practice. The numbers of false positives and false negatives provide an indication of the inaccuracy of an algorithm. Approximate algorithms are very common in Informatics. A very important reason is that there are many problems that are undecidable. An *undecidable problem* is a decision problem for which it is impossible to construct an algorithm that always leads to a correct (yes/no) answer.

Undecidable problems are ubiquitous. In particular, most problems concerning program analysis are undecidable. Program analysis refers to automatic techniques, which analyze computer programs to verify certain properties that assure absence of bugs in the program, or to exclude the occurrence of certain suspicious looking conditions.

A very simple property may be: "every statement in the program is executable", meaning that it is reachable by the execution flow in some feasible computation. A statement that is never executed is useless: it constitutes so-called "dead code".[11] Although a well-written program should not contain dead code, per se it does not indicate an error in the program. However, it is very often the symptom that there is an error in the program. An algorithm that produces the list of all unreachable statements would be quite useful in program debugging. Unfortunately, this problem is undecidable, and an exact algorithm does not exist. Program analysis research has studied this problem and has produced approximate solutions. A sound solution would produce a list of statements that are guaranteed to be unreachable (although there can be more). A complete solution would produce a list of statements that includes all unreachable statements, although some of them might instead be reachable. Notice that an algorithm that always produces an empty set of statements would be sound, while an algorithm that always produces all statements would be complete. However, in these two cases the number of false negatives and false positives, respectively, would be unacceptably high!

---

[11] A very special (and important) case is reachability of the termination statement of a program. If the termination statement is unreachable, the program never terminates.

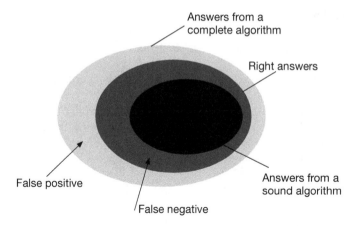

Fig. 2.3 Sound and complete algorithms, false positives and false negatives. The grey set indicates the set of right answers for the problem; the dark grey set indicates the set of answers computed by a sound algorithm; the light grey set indicates the set of answers computed by a complete algorithm. Elements in the intersection between the light grey set and the grey set are false positives. Elements in the intersection between the grey set and the dark grey set are false negatives

As another example, consider an image recognition algorithm that is supposed to detect photographs that contain cats. Given a set of n photographs, m of which are known to contain cats, the algorithm may recognize as containing cats k of them, and may recognize additional h photos containing furry animals that are not cats. The fraction

$$k/(k+h) \qquad (2.4)$$

indicates the *precision* of the algorithm on the given set of photographs. If it equal to 1, all detected pictures do contain cats. Instead, the fraction

$$k/m \qquad (2.5)$$

which is called *recall*, indicates the completeness of the computed solutions. If it is equal to 1, all photos containing cats are detected.

Precision and recall are two extremely useful notions to assess adequacy of an approximate algorithm. In the previous example, we computed them on a sample input—a set of photos that may or may not contain humans. To generalize from a single case to any set of photos, we would need to set up an experimental assessment in which we use various data sets of photos. This may lead to an *estimate* of precision and recall for the given algorithm.

Precision and recall may be formally defined as follows. Let tp, fp, fn be the number of true positive, false positives, and false negatives, respectively. *Precision* p is defined as:

$$p = tp/(tp+fp) \qquad (2.6)$$

Recall r is defined as:

$$r = tp/(tp + fn) \tag{2.7}$$

Ideally, p and r should be both equal to 1. A sound algorithm has precision 1, while a complete algorithm has recall 1.

In general, precision and recall of a decision algorithm can be evaluated experimentally. The experimental setting requires executing the algorithm on a statistically representative input data set on which the algorithm is validated. It also requires an *oracle*, which can assess whether the output is a true positive, a false positive, or a false negative.

2.5   Further Discussion on Validation of Research Results

Researchers have the responsibility to provide evidence of validity of what they claim to be research results. Validation is predominantly achieved by experimental assessment. From the previous discussion and examples, we can conclude that this is certainly true in the case of analytic research, which aims at understanding real-world phenomena by formulating a theory that explains them. The theory is mainly validated through experiments. How is validation performed in other kinds of research? What is the role of experimentation? This is the goal of the discussion presented in this section.

In formal research, validation is mostly done in a different way. Results are often stated as theorems and the research contribution mainly lies in the difficulty, subtlety, and elegance of the mathematical proof, which may require deep mathematical skills and ingenuity by the researcher. As an example in Informatics, a research may lead to the proof of complexity of a certain algorithm, or the computational power of a certain formalism. As we observed earlier, validation of complex theorems proved by a scientist undergoes a social process of continuous scrutiny that can improve confidence [7]. This process is a kind of proof-of-time, experimental validation. Conjectured theorems are also often challenged through test data before a proof is attempted. If the test fails, there is no sense in attempting a proof. The test represents a counter-example to the conjecture. Counter-examples are indeed examples of an experimental attitude in mathematical research. Carefully chosen "experiments" (i.e., counter-examples) can be used to falsify a statement. A proof by counterexample is a way of to show that a given universal statement cannot possibly be correct by showing an instance that contradicts the statement. The identification of a counter-example can sometimes provide hints to the researcher on how to restate the theorem in a more appropriate form that eliminates the counter-example.

Let us consider the case of constructive research. Suppose that the output of a research is an artifact that solves an important problem. For example, it may be an algorithm that computes an exact solution for the problem. In this case, validation consists of providing evidence that (a) the solution is correct and (b) the algorithm has an acceptable complexity and can be executed in an acceptable time for its possible uses. In the previous section, we have also seen the case of algorithmic artifacts that provide approximate solutions to problems for which an exact solution does not exist, or would not be practically usable. In these cases, validation should assess whether the approximation is acceptable. That is, the effect of possible false positives and false negatives is tolerable in practical use. In most cases, exhaustive validation of the artifact is out of question, since the input space to explore is too large or even infinite. Validation must be done through experiments, which sample the problem space in a statistically significant way.

Constructive research may also develop completely new artifacts that do things we could not do before, or do things in a new and better way. For example, consider research that develops a new tool supporting cooperative design of intelligent buildings or research that investigates the use of computer games to help children learn mathematics. Validation of these kinds of artifacts becomes more elusive. It may consist in demonstrating the effectiveness or the performance of a proposed artifact, or its efficient use of resources with respect to previously known results. It may instead insist on reliability of the solutions computed by an artifact and their robustness with respect to certain changes. Researchers need to provide evidence that the artifact is built on rigorous grounds, it is novel, and it is significant.

We wish to focus hereafter on two questions. First, how can we choose a validation strategy? And second, how do we ensure that validation is done properly?

As for the first question, the validation strategy varies a lot across different kinds of research. For example, in Physics or in Biology, researchers may need to set up experiments in laboratory. Physics research in some cases requires building ad-hoc very expensive experimental facilities. Experimental facilities can be also very expensive in Engineering research, for example requiring a wind tunnel to assess certain fluid-dynamics conditions of a new aircraft.

In Informatics, but also in social sciences and in life sciences, experiments can take the form of case studies. A *case study* is a research validation effort involving an up-close, in-depth, and detailed examination of a subject of study (the case), as well as its related contextual conditions. A case study may concern the use of a proposed new artifact in a given context, or the effectiveness of an approximate algorithm in given operational conditions.

A case study may be real or simulated. A simulated case study may be implemented in a simulation software environment, where possible validation situations may be generated according to different stochastic policies. The advantage of a simulated case study is that huge numbers of different situations can be generated. For example, simulation may provide an accurate analysis of precision and recall of an approximate algorithm, assuming that the right answers are known. The disadvantage is that normally simulation implies an abstraction of the real setting, which may oversimplify the case and make it unrealistic. To overcome some of these problems, often a case study is partly simulated and partly real.

The purpose of a case study may be to observe the case, extract data from the observation, and analyze whether and how the data conform to the expectations. An *observational case study* may for example allow a researcher to show that a novel artifact performs well in a variety of use conditions, possibly in a real setting. Sometimes the scope is even more restricted. A *feasibility case study* (or *pilot case study*) may simply have the goal to demonstrate that a given proposed solution is feasible and has potential. This is sometimes a prerequisite for further research that may then lead to more proper validation. A *comparative case study* is done mainly to compare a research outcome against competitors. It normally assumes that a common checklist exists against which the comparison can be made. An important example is a *community case study* (or *benchmark*). A community case is created by certain research communities to launch competitions among researchers working in a certain area to address a certain case; for example, automatic solvers of logic formulae, or document retrieval tools.

An important property of a validation is that it must be replicable.[12] Anybody should be able to reproduce the exact conditions under which certain results were obtained, and the same results should be obtained. A *replicability case study* has exactly the purpose of reproducing the experiments anew. In many fields, replicability case studies are key to improving confidence in the validity of research findings. Sometimes the goal may be to assess how the experiment remains valid while certain conditions change, or what changes in the experiment when certain conditions change.

Experiments made to validate research results may fall under the category of *controlled experiments*. These are very common when the subjects of the experiment are humans, as frequently happens in social sciences and in medicine. It may also happen in constructive research to validate the effects of using a given artifact in performing certain activities. A controlled experiment is a research study in which the subjects are randomly assigned to two groups, and the goal of the experiment is to determine cause and effect between variables. More precisely, the subjects of the experiment are divided into an *experimental group* and a *control group*. The experimental group is a group of individuals who are exposed to the factor being examined. The control group is not exposed to the factor. Because the goal of the experiment is to validate the hypothesis that the factor causes a certain effect, it is imperative that all other possible factors are held constant between the experimental group and the control group. The only factor that is different between the two groups is the one being investigated. Random assignment of participants to the two groups is done in order to ensure that participants are not assigned in a way that could bias the study results.

Once again, it is important to stress the intrinsic limits to the validity of research findings assessed by even very carefully conducted controlled experiments. Research findings are rarely expressed as absolute truths. This makes it very hard to convey the notion of validity of a scientific statement to the general public,

---

[12]More on this is discussed in Sect. 3.6.

and in particular to properly communicate scientific findings that touch highly sensitive issues, as happens for example in the medical field. Box 2.9 discusses these implications in the case of epidemiological studies on vaccines.

Let us now focus on the second question: which criteria can be adopted to ensure that validation is done properly? To answer to this question, we need to consider that there are two sides of this problem. First, we need to explicitly, precisely, and unambiguously state what is the *validation question*. In a very generic form, in the case of analytic research, the question might be: does my hypothesis X properly describe phenomenon Y? Of course, the question would need to be broken up into more concrete and specific questions. Examples of research questions are: "can a certain drug D cause a certain effect E on patients?", or "does this novel technique implemented by an artifact help programmers in debugging?", or "is the approximation provided by this incomplete and unsound algorithm acceptable when applied in a certain context?" Very often, the research question takes the form of a causal relation: "does X cause Y"? The first two previous examples describe causal relations.

Proper validation also requires that we explicitly focus on the *validation answer*, i.e., on the definition and implementation of the experimental setting and on the data we observe and collect, which are supposed to answer the validation question. A proper validation requires *internal validity*. Internal validity (validity inside the case) means that validation strongly supports the validation question and rules out alternative hypotheses. Consider the case where the validation question is expressed as a causal relation—*A causes B*. Experiments need to show that manifestations of phenomenon A (say, $a_1, a_2, \ldots, a_i$) are correlated with respective manifestations of B (say, $b_1, b_2, \ldots b_i$). Evidence of correlation, however, is not sufficient to claim causality. We would also need to ensure that the manifestations of B only occur if their causes in A have occurred before in time (time precedence) and there are no plausible alternative explanations for the observed covariation. To support internal validity, researchers need to perform a careful *threat analysis*, to identify all possible circumstances that might weaken the validation. Analysis of threats to internal validity is a prerequisite for validation and is an argument that must be discussed to support the findings when a researcher decides to publish a research result.

The notion of *external validity* (validity outside the case) is also quite useful. It defines the extent to which the observed results from validation can be generalized to other contexts. For instance, how do the results from a case study apply to other possible case studies? As an example, consider a research question concerning usability of a new tool supporting cooperative document development, which was validated by observing usage of the tool by college students, collecting data, and drawing conclusions. Can the findings be generalized to other classes of users, for example, professionals collecting requirements for the development of a complex and critical system?

Box 2.9: Do Vaccines Cause Autism?

A heated debate was brought to the general public in the late 1990s, questioning vaccines as a cause of autism in children, especially after a claim was made that the measles-mumps-rubella (MMR) vaccine would cause autism. Controlled experiments involving two groups (autistic and non-autistic individuals) could provide no scientific support to this claim. As we have long discussed, when scientists conclude that there is "no evidence", the statement should not be confused as an absolute truth. This may lead to a difficult situation when scientists engage in discussions with the general public. To shed light on this issue, I would like to provide a long quote from the vivid and passionate words of P.A. Offit in his book "Bad Advice: Or Why Celebrities, Politicians, and Activists Aren't Your Best Source of Health Information" [38].

> "Scientists learn that the scientific method doesn't allow for absolute certainty. When scientists formulate a hypothesis, it's always framed in the negative; this is known as the null hypothesis. When communicating science to the public, the null hypothesis can be a problem.
>
> I'll give you an example. Suppose you want to know whether the measles-mumps-rubella (MMR) vaccine causes autism. The null hypothesis would be *the MMR vaccine does not cause autism*. Studies designed to answer this question can result in two possible outcomes. Findings can reject the null hypothesis, meaning that autism following the MMR vaccine occurs at a level greater than would be expected by chance alone. Or, findings cannot reject the null hypothesis, meaning that autism following the MMR vaccine occurs at a level expected by chance alone. The temptation in the first case would be to say that the MMR vaccine causes autism and in the second that it doesn't. But scientists can't make either of those statements. They can only say that one thing is associated with another at a certain level of statistical probability.
>
> Also, scientists can never accept the null hypothesis; said another way, they can never prove never.
>
>   . . .
>
> One example of how the scientific method can enslave scientists occurred in front of the House of Representatives Committee on Government Reform. On April 6, 2000, a Republican member of Congress from Indiana, Dan Burton, certain that the MMR vaccine had caused his grandson's autism, held a hearing to air his ill-founded belief. At the time, one study had already shown that children who had received the MMR vaccine had the same risk of autism as those who hadn't received it. (Since that hearing, sixteen additional studies have found the same thing.) The scientists who testified at the hearing, however, knew that no scientific study could ever prove that the MMR vaccine does not cause autism. They knew they could never say, *The MMR vaccine doesn't cause autism.* So they didn't. Rather, they said things like, *All the evidence to date doesn't support the hypothesis that the MMR vaccine causes autism.* To Dan Burton, this sounded like a door was being left open—like the scientists were waffling or worse, covering something up."

2.6 Conclusions

This chapter investigated research methods. It started with a historical retrospective analysis of the contributions from the scientific revolution in the seventeenth century, which originated what became known as the experimental method. Often in schools students are taught that science progresses through a rational, ordered sequence of events, whose driver is the scientific method. This idealized view is very far from reality. Scientific research is driven by creativity, on one side, and rigorous and systematic methods for the description and validation of research results, on the other. The interplay between the two forces leads to an evolving, non-linear process. In addition, creativity is at least partially conducive to disordered or even chaotic processes. Some people say jokingly that research is partly *inspiration* and partly *perspiration*. They are both important and none of them should be underestimated. Although research must be ignited by a creative act (inspiration), most of the effort then goes into clarifying, rationalizing, formalizing, and validating creations (perspiration).

Likewise, research does not necessarily lead to ground-braking results. Most of the time, it builds incrementally on previous work. The interplay of revolutionary steps and incremental progress (between paradigm shifts and "normal science", according to [31], is what generates the continuous, collective research progress. Bertrand Meyer [35] provides an interesting discussion of the value of incremental research in Informatics.

This chapter has shown that there are several approaches to research, rather than a single blanket standard method, which can be used to drive and validate research. It focused on the methods used in Physical sciences and Engineering, especially referring to those used in Informatics. Other approaches may also be found in other disciplines. For example, *action research* is a common research method in social sciences, where research is done in a collaborative way while driving personal and organizational changes. Researchers may need to go deeper into specific methods of their research by looking at the specialized literature.

2.7 Further Reading

For a general discussion of research methodology, the reader may refer to [44]. For a specific discussion of research methods in constructive research, the reader might refer to [65]. This book provides an excellent coverage of research that focuses on artifact design, also called "Design Science." The science of Informatics is discussed specifically in [9, 57, 61].

The book on the Vienna circle [52] is highly recommended for readers who are interested in the historical roots of modern philosophy of science. The book provides a fascinating portrait of an extraordinary group of intellectuals in the early twentieth century who transformed the way we now think about science.

For a deeper and critical understanding of the contributions from philosophy of science, the reader might refer to [17], which provides an excellent coverage of the field. One might also directly access the essays by influential science philosophers, like K. Popper [43], T. Kuhn [31], P. Feyerabend [14].

Chapter 3
The Products of Research: Publication and Beyond

This chapter focuses on the products of research. Like any other process, research produces results, which are disseminated to those who may have an interest in them: other researchers, industry, society at large. Research products are primarily new knowledge that is made available in the form of scientific publications. However, other forms of dissemination are also important, like oral presentations in specialized technical meetings or to a general audience. Dissemination also occurs indirectly through people, like students, who participate in research activities and then move to industry, or researchers who spin-off to industry their results. Hereafter I mainly focus on dissemination through scientific papers: how to write papers, how papers get reviewed before publication, and more generally how the publishing world works. I also discuss other forms of dissemination that are becoming more and more relevant, such as prototypes, software packages, data sets, and videos. They are also collectively called *artifacts*.

The focus of this chapter is on the *process* through which research products are diffused. Evaluation of research products is an essential aspect of the process. It is extensively discussed separately in Chap. 5.

This chapter is organized as follows. Section 3.1 discusses what is a research result and when it deserves being disseminated. Section 3.2 focuses on scientific papers published in journals and conferences. Paper writing principles and writing tips are presented in Sect. 3.3. The peer review process that leads to publishable papers is examined in Sect. 3.4, while the broader context of the publication world is illustrated in Sect. 3.5. Other forms of dissemination of research results are examined in Sect. 3.6. After discussing the emerging open science approach in Sect. 3.7, some concluding remarks on diffusion of research products are given in Sect. 3.8.

© Springer Nature Switzerland AG 2020
C. Ghezzi, *Being a Researcher*, https://doi.org/10.1007/978-3-030-45157-8_3

3.1 What Is a Research Result?

Let us ask again the key question: what is a research result and why and when it deserves diffusion? A result is a unit of knowledge or a particular artifact that was not available before and can be of interest for others, who may enrich their stock of knowledge or tools and use them to further advance research or practice. During the research process, one may produce several results. A result may be a novel solution of a problem faced by the researcher, an improvement of existing solutions to an important problem, or a generalization of a previously known theory. Each of these may be of interest to other researchers who are working on the same or a similar problem.

The next question is why research results are disseminated. I would say that dissemination is connatural to research. Research is a collective social effort, and scientists working in the same area naturally share their results. They benefit from the results of their peers and can build on top of them with new contributions that advance progress in an area. Research aims at generating new knowledge and progress in society. It is primarily funded by public investments which require openness. Any limitations to diffusion, sometimes imposed by the funding source (for example, in the case of industry funding), are typically viewed by researchers as limitations to their freedom.

A further question I wish to address is: When do we have a result that is ready and warrants diffusion? This mainly boils down to the further questions: Is this result of interest to others? Does it have enough intellectual depth? Is it in a state that allows whoever may be interested to benefit from it? To answer these questions, we may once again refer to the three main attributes of a research product we discussed earlier in Chap. 1, namely:

- originality;
- rigor;
- significance.

Recall that originality means that the product provides new insights. In the case of a paper, it describes novel results which were not known before. Rigor refers to the intellectual integrity of the research process and the way the results are demonstrated or justified. In the case of analytic research, this refers to the way experimental data are collected and analyzed to confirm the findings. For formal research, it may refer to the rigor of mathematical apparatus—definitions, proofs—used to describe the findings. In the case of constructive research, it may refer to the constructive principles used to design an artifact and in the assessment of its potential use. Significance means that the results of research have enough intellectual depth to exert, or have the potential to exert, an influence: on other research, on industry, or on society.

Originality, rigor, and significance are not binary attributes. A research result may have high or low originality, significance, and rigor. Originality, significance, and rigor are also relative to the specific audience to which the product is directed. They are also relative to the kind of research product. If a result is presented to a highly specialized research audience, the rigor must be higher than in the case where the audience mainly consists of practitioners. Conversely, practitioners may be more interested in the empirical data gathered from realistic case studies. Likewise, consider the case where the research product is a survey paper. We expect it to score lower in originality than a paper describing a novel result. In this case, originality may lie mainly in the method used for the survey or in the absence of similar surveys for the topic. A survey may be quite significant because it may offer a well reasoned and systematic analysis of the state of the art in a given area. To deserve diffusion, a product should be scored beyond a minimum threshold in all the three dimensions and score well in at least one. The researcher should responsibly self-assess the readiness of the product with respect to originality, significance and rigor, before diffusing it to a given target audience.

3.2 Research Papers

This section focuses on dissemination of research results through scientific papers. This is still the primary way of communicating science in most fields. Writing a paper is an offspring of the research process. Results are produced incrementally; they are continuously revised and refined. During this process, they are accumulated in various forms (manual sketches, mathematical formulae and proof outlines, preliminary concept implementations, execution results of computer simulations, experimental data, interviews, and so on). They are progressively collected, organized, and written down in a coherent textual document. The act of selecting, writing down, polishing, and systematizing the material collected throughout the research journey is first of all crucial for the researcher herself. We would never be able to guarantee any level of assurance of a research result until we try to spell it out in a systematic, rigorous, and detailed manner. I would even say that we really know what we are talking about only after we put our thoughts together and write them down precisely.

To validate certain steps of research, often researchers write *internal reports* that are not even supposed to be published as scientific papers. They only serve an internal purpose in the research process: shedding light on all aspects of the research to achieve confidence in its coherence. Internal reports are mainly work-in-progress papers that may have an exclusive internal use within the research group, or may have limited and controlled distribution. Their goal is to solicit feedback from a selected external audience.

Once a research has matured, papers are written to be disseminated openly as publications. The term publication comes from Latin "publicare", which means "make public": research results are made public, open to others. The process of writing a scientific paper for publication is a laborious and time-consuming process. It is never done in one shot, but rather through continuous revisions. Publications may be developed from the internal reports we just mentioned, from initial drafts, or from other working material. By publishing a research paper, researchers take

responsibility for its contents. Their reputation and stand in a research community
depend on their publications. Since researchers must be proud of their research
results, before opening them to the public they should do their best to ensure that the
paper has intellectual depth and makes a valuable contribution: the work is original
and significant, and the results are obtained and described in a rigorous way.

There are two kinds of publications. The first is through a medium that only
ensures visibility of the contribution to the general public. Today, this is achieved
via electronic archives. The simplest way is to use a personal archive (for example
via a personal web page). There are also public archives, like arXiv, that can be used
for this purpose. We come back to this later.

The most important way of publishing research results, however, is through
publication venues that are based on *peer review*. Peer review, which is discussed
in detail in Sect. 3.4, is a cornerstone of the research eco-system. In the context of
publication, it means that a paper is disclosed to the public only after experts in the
field (peers) review it, to verify that it reaches a given quality threshold. Peer review
acts as a validation filter that aims at preventing publication of papers that do not
meet certain scholarly standards. It provides a kind of certification that the paper has
scientific value and it is worth being published. It may also provide suggestions for
changes that may improve the quality of the published work.

Since publications are research products, it is inevitable to use them to derive an
approximate measure of productivity and quality of a researcher. This is especially
true for peer-reviewed publications, since they carry a third-party certification. This
use has generated in researchers a tension towards publication that often goes
beyond the natural and legitimate aspiration to disclose research results. It has
generated a confusion between quantity of research outputs and their quality, which
is the ultimate goal. "Publish or perish" is a phrase that has been coined and is often
used to describe this pressure on researchers. It is important to stress, however,
that the goal of research is to advance science and produce interesting and useful
results: publication is only one of the means to achieve these goals, not the end. We
come back to this problem with more discussion in Chap. 5, which focuses on the
evaluation of research and researchers.

Scientific journals are traditionally and in general the most widely used peer-
reviewed publication venues. All research areas have a set of reference journals. Of
those, some are considered as prestigious venues by the researchers who are active in
the area. Publishing a paper in those journals is viewed by the research community,
and by the individual researcher, as a major achievement. A venue is viewed as
prestigious because the research community working in the area considers it as
such: it has a long history of influential contributed articles, the editorial process to
accept contributions is severe and thorough, the editors and reviewers are respected
scientists in the area, and so on. Researchers try to publish their best results in
top journals, which serve as authoritative research archives. In each area, there
are also less prestigious, second-tier journals, sometimes specialized on specific
sub-topics, which may be the target publication of research results that are not
considered to reach the quality threshold set by the top archival journals. Selecting
the most appropriate publication target for a research result is an important decision

researchers have to make. The way a result should be presented depends on the requirements and the style of papers commonly accepted by a venue.

Scientific conferences can also be peer-reviewed publication venues. In certain areas, such as Informatics, they are considered to be equally valid target venues as journals, and sometimes they even have a higher profile. However, this is often not true for other scientific areas. There are areas where contributions to conferences are not peer-reviewed, or they are only subject to a very lightweight screening. There are also cases where speakers are invited to present, but they are not even asked to submit written contributions.

In Informatics, each specific sub-area (e.g., software engineering or computer vision) has its own reference conferences, some of which are considered as very prestigious. The reason why conferences are so prominent in Informatics is that the area has been evolving at an extremely high speed, and conferences became more effective dissemination media than journals, because they ensure a faster and predictable process from submission to publication. Journals instead typically require a longer editorial process before publication.[1] Conferences have a submission date within which contributions must be submitted, a fixed period for review, and a known date when decision about acceptance or rejection is made and communicated to the authors. These dates are hard time constraints that journals do not usually have. Like journals, conferences can belong to different prestige tiers, and one should carefully select the conference that best fits the topic and the research result to be presented.

The choice of a possible publication target venue should never be guided by a criterion that favors the low bar set for acceptance. In recent years, there has been a proliferation of journals of questionable quality and dubious reputation, which offer easy publication opportunities. As for journals, researchers should beware of dubious quality conferences. They should always be avoided. Wasting precious time to publish in third-tier venues, just because more serious venues are difficult, is always a bad choice. Even worse, there are *predatory publishers* (see Box 3.1), who actively look for papers to publish in journals or conferences, with only very limited or even no review process. Sometimes they charge authors a publication fee. Publication in these venues must be carefully avoided, since it may damage the image of the researchers who publish in them. Unfortunately, this is one of the negative consequences of the obsession towards publication I mentioned earlier.

Before closing this section, I wish to stress again that writing papers is a laborious and time consuming task. Beginning researchers often underestimate it. This issue becomes extremely critical when paper submissions are subject to hard

---

[1]Some journals have been investing considerable efforts to try to counter this phenomenon and compete with the conferences that decide about acceptance/rejection in three to 4 months.

> ### Box 3.1: Predatory Publishers
>
> To exemplify what predatory journal publishers do, I report an anonymized
> verbatim invitation from one of them. Invitations of this kind are extremely
> common: sadly, this is just an example of the many email invitations
> received by researchers, as potential targets of recruitment by predatory
> publishers. Even more sadly, predatory publishers count on inexperienced
> researchers to fall inadvertently in these traps.
>
> > International Journal of XXX
> > Dear Ghezzi, C
> > Warm greetings from the editorial office! We have learnt about your precious
> > paper titled [...] which has been published in [...], and the topic of the paper has
> > impressed us a lot. It has drawn attention and interest from researchers working in
> > Wireless sensor networks; software adaptation; context-oriented programming.[2]
> > Submit Your Research Papers to the Journal of XXX. Initiated with an aim to
> > advance the development of scientific community, International Journal of XXX
> > can make specialists in various domains closer to the cutting-edge researches
> > around the world. In light of the advance, novelty, and potential extensive
> > application of your research achievements, we invite you to send other unpublished
> > works of similar themes to the journal. Your latest research of this published article
> > is also welcomed. Refer to the link below to learn more: http://www.ZZZ.org/
> > submission
>
> The e-mail continues offering the recipient to join the Editorial Board.
>
> > On behalf of the Editorial Board of the journal, we are very pleased to invite you
> > to join our team as one of the editorial board members of International Journal
> > of XXX. Your academic background and rich experience in this field are highly
> > appreciated by us. We believe that this opportunity will promote international
> > academic collaborations in the future. If you have any interest to join us, please
> > visit: http://www.ZZZ.org/joinus
>
> Predatory publishers also organize conferences. For example, I have even
> been invited as a speaker in a conference pompously titled "World Congress
> on Advanced Materials." The invitation was extended to me because of my
> "outstanding contribution regarding. "piezoelectric materials, ..." Notice
> that my research area has nothing to do with Advanced Materials, let alone
> Piezoelectric Materials! Of course, I would have needed to register for the
> conference, and pay a registration fee.

deadlines, as happens with conferences. Underestimating the effort may lead to
missing submission opportunities. Writing is hard since the author needs to move
from informal concepts and ideas into rational, systematic, rigorous, and polished
descriptions.

---

[2]This is just a random list of buzzwords, probably automatically extracted from my previous
papers.

3.3 Paper Writing Principles and Practical Tips

Writing scientific papers requires special skills. Books are available and courses are offered on scientific writing, to equip scientists with the necessary principles and guidelines. Although this is not the primary topic of the book, this section highlights some principles an author of a research paper should follow, along with some practical tips. For an in-depth treatment of technical writing, the reader should refer to the specialized literature.

The golden principle one should follow is: start writing only after you have

- clearly spelled out the goals you wish to achieve, and
- carefully planned what you intend to say as a logical flow of discourse.

This golden principle has a general validity that goes beyond technical paper writing. Understanding the requirements and planning the development should always precede the actual implementation of any activity. This is, for example, a well-known principle in engineering endeavors: it reduces the risks of failures and guarantees quality. In the case of paper writing, after deciding that a research result warrants publication, a researcher should indeed focus first on the *message* he wants to convey through the paper. The message should be a convincing argument which highlights the paper's contribution. It can be of the form "I solved the long-standing problem X", or "I demonstrated the improved performance in executing task Y through the use of the novel technique Z", "I report the results of an observational study of the positive effect of using technique W in context T." The paper should then stay aligned with the goal. Through the paper, the author needs to convince the reader that the problem is novel and significant and that it has been solved in a rigorous way. The paper itself should be well written and rigorous.

The message to be conveyed has to be chosen and calibrated by taking into account to whom the message is directed (the expected *stakeholders*). Considering the previous examples, if the message is "I solved the standing problem X", one should understand who is affected by the proposed solution, and who is interested (and why) in knowing the solution. Likewise, if the message is "I demonstrated the improved performance in performing task Y through the use of technique Z", one should understand who may take advantage of the improvement, and who may be interested in the technique. Understanding the stakeholders means that one understands the audience to which the paper is directed. A researcher writes a paper for a certain conference with a specific focus and attendance. If the paper is going to be submitted to a journal, one should understand the style of the papers appearing in the journal, which is what its readership expects.

Planning a paper amounts to deciding what one will say and in which order. If this is done properly, the readers are guided by a rigorous, cohesive, logical structure which makes the contribution understandable. While writing, a researcher should not follow his own stream of consciousness, nor ramble on different issues. Two conflicting issues arise in the planning phase: the amount and level of details to be included, on the one side, and the constraint on length of submissions, on the other. Length may be a hard constraint, since most conferences and journals only give authors a limited page budget, and may immediately reject submissions exceeding the budget. It may be a soft constraint, in cases where the page limit is only recommended, but not strictly enforced. Even in this case, however, one cannot go beyond a reasonable length. Conciseness and focus on the essentials are important, otherwise readers can be discouraged by a lengthy contribution that may contain too many things. In deciding what should go in, one should remember that the purpose is to communicate a specific contribution, and everything in the paper should be directed to this goal. If any part of the paper does not do so, it should be deleted. Everything in the paper that does not support the main point distracts from it. The author should always remember that the paper is directed to others, not to herself. Details that the author finds most intriguing and mostly fulfill self-accomplishment should be eliminated.

While planning the structure, the author should focus on the contribution, rather than describe the history of what the author has done. The author should be guided by the message to convey, not by the historical process through which the result has been reached, which is often not relevant. Reporting that the research went through trials and errors often only has an anecdotal value. Only in some cases, trials and errors may also be of interest to others and may be worth publishing, to shed light on pathways that apparently look promising, but instead lead to dead ends. This may prevent others from trying demonstrably wrong approaches in the future.

Although the main goal of the paper is to highlight its contribution, it must also provide an adequate context. It should tell the reader which are the necessary premises and assumptions upon which the contribution is based. Furthermore, it must tell the reader how the results have been challenged and validated. Finally, it should situate the contribution in the context of the state of the art and related work. A reference structure of a standard research paper is described in the Box 3.2.

As a last remark, one should never forget that, despite careful planning of the structure, paper writing inevitably undergoes several iterations. In the initial iterations, the tendency is to add material. Later iterations instead focus on polishing: simplification and elimination of material.

3.4   The Peer Review Process

Research is a social process that is mainly self-managed by researchers. Researchers produce results that other researchers may use to generate further progress. They participate in the assessment of the work by other researchers and drive the publication process. The path that leads a research paper submitted to a conference or a journal through the review process and to the decision whether it should be published is entirely in the hands of peer researchers. *Peer review* is crucial to guarantee scientific progress. It aims at preventing dissemination of poor or flawed research outputs. This filter is vital to avoid flooding the research community with inaccurate, wrong, or irrelevant material, and reducing noise. Peer review is

Box 3.2: Paper Writing Tips

Scientific papers follow a pretty standard syntactic organization, whose main elements are described here. The *front matter* consists of title and author list, with affiliations, and abstract. The *title* must be short and informative. It must capture the attention of potential readers. The *abstract* is a crucial piece of text. It must be short, often a single paragraph, and yet it must convey the message in a condensed form. Most readers decide to read a paper only if the abstract motivates them to continue reading. It must clearly state the relevance of the problem, the proposed solution, and how it is justified.

The *body* of the paper often follows a standard structure:

1. Introduction. This is perhaps the most important section. If the abstract is an invitation to read the paper, the introduction must convey an overall view of the contribution, and in particular its rationale. The rest of the paper then justifies it by providing the necessary details. Usually a reader forms an opinion about the paper after reading the introduction. This is also true for reviewers. The decision to accept or reject the paper matures after reading the introduction, and gets confirmed by the details provided in the other sections. The introduction should clearly contain the following information: what is the problem addressed in the paper, why the problem is important/difficult/interesting, what is lacking in the current knowledge about the problem, what is the novel contribution, and how its validity is supported. A brief outline of the rest of the paper may also be useful.

2. Background. This section may recall the main pieces of background knowledge needed by the reader to understand the details of the contribution, as well as existing work the paper builds upon.

3. Problem statement and proposed solution. This section provides a detailed description of the technical contribution. Often this can done by using a running example, which should be simple and easy to follow. This makes the treatment more concrete and easier to understand.

4. Validity of the contribution. This section describes how the findings have been validated, through one or more of the different techniques discussed earlier in Sect. 2.5.

5. Related work. This section has a different purpose than the background section. Its purpose is to compare and contrast the paper's contribution to competing related work. If comparison to related work affects the validity of the proposed solution, this section may precede the previous.

6. Conclusions. This section restates the main findings of the research, their possible implications, strengths and weaknesses, and outlines possible future work.

The above standard structure is generic. Its purpose is mainly to shed light on the flow of arguments that should be addressed. In practice, titles for the sections should be more informative and problem specific. Additional sections may also be introduced, and sections may be structured through subsections. For each section, it may be useful to start with a mini-introduction that says its purpose and its organization.

also essential to guide improvement of submitted material before its diffusion and thus potentially improve its impact. Peer reviewers are recognized experts who voluntarily accept to act as reviewers. They are expected to invest their experience, knowledge, and integrity as a service contribution to the research community. Reviewing papers should be considered by researchers as a *moral obligation* to contribute to the health of the research community. A self-managed community relies on the fact that its members spend part of their time and put their best energies into supporting it. Scientists get benefit from peer review, both directly and indirectly. The main direct benefit is improvement of own work before it goes public. The main indirect benefit is noise reduction due to filtering of worthless material.

Peer review is a pillar upon which the world of research is founded. It has been key to advancing science. It is a very atypical and fragile process, subject to threats. It works on a purely voluntary basis, which means that no central authority can ultimately steer it. It is also very expensive: researchers spend quite a lot of their time in reviewing. Unfortunately, the efforts spent remain quite invisible and do not receive much public recognition. The motivation to work thoroughly on reviews is largely purely ethical. This explains the other side of the coin: why researchers can be reluctant to engage in reviewing, and also why sometimes reviews are done poorly. The situation becomes even more critical in research areas that are developing very quickly and attract many researchers—a typical example in recent years is machine learning. Conferences and journals cannot find a sufficient number of expert reviewers who can assist in reviewing the massive flow of incoming submissions. When huge numbers of submissions are involved, acceptance or rejection become more like the results of a lottery than objective scientific decisions.

Pitfalls of peer review can have severe consequences. Since it is often easier to find minor flaws than support novel ideas, good papers which do not follow the mainstream fashion may be rejected. This may prevent timely dissemination of significant research breakthroughs. Likewise, there have been experiments by researchers to show how poorly peer review is sometimes practiced and how ineffective it can be in detecting unscientific contributions. In 1996, Alan Sokal, a physics professor at New York University and University College London, published a paper in a leading North American journal of cultural studies, which admittedly was a hoax. In 2005, three MIT students created "SCIgen", a program that randomly generates nonsensical computer-science papers, complete with realistic-looking graphs, figures, and citations. Their goal was to reveal the unfortunate diffusion of unscrupulous peer-review practices, especially by predatory publishers. The authors indeed had a computer-generated paper accepted by conference that was officially sponsored by a professional society.

These are extreme examples, which cannot be generalized to shed a negative light on the value of peer review. Peer review is still the most effective way we know to sustain research dissemination, and the research community should continue to invest its best efforts to support and enhance its integrity and effectiveness. It is fair to say, however, that despite all the efforts invested in it, peer review is far from being perfect: it does not prevent poor or even flawed papers from being published.

The ultimate assessment of validity of published work is a social process of scrutiny that continues over time and involves the entire community.

Let us look closer to how peer reviewing fits into the publication process by focusing on journal papers. What I say here holds, with possible small variations, for most scientific journals. A journal has an *editorial board* (associate editors), headed by an *editor-in-chief*, who is responsible for the definition and implementation of the scientific strategy, ranging from the identification of the topics of interest to the quality standards required for publication, the management of the review process, and its integrity.

When a paper is submitted for publication, the editor-in-chief assigns it to a member of the editorial board, who is then responsible for further processing. The editor selects possible reviewers, who report to her. Associate editors and reviewers are the main actors of the peer-review process. The members of the editorial board of respectable journals are chosen among internationally known and respected researchers with a broad experience in the subject areas covered by the journal. Serving on the editorial board of a prestigious journal is considered by researchers as a sign of distinction. Reviewers are selected among experts in the topic of the paper. They are expected to be aware of the requirements stated by the journal, in particular the expected quality standards to be met by submissions. Very often, they are chosen among previous successful contributors. When they accept to review a paper, they are expected to dedicate adequate time and effort into the task and to produce a detailed and well-motivated assessment. Most importantly, to ensure fairness of the peer-review process, all involved reviewers (editor in charge of the paper and reviewers) should have no *conflict of interest* with the authors and should apply fair, unbiased, and constructive judgement.[3]

The typical workflow of the editorial process of journal submissions is shown in Fig. 3.1. Before selecting the reviewers, the editor checks for appropriateness of the submission—for example in terms of length or formatting—and as a result may decide to desk reject it (for example, as out of scope or for evident lack of technical contents). Otherwise, she searches for appropriate reviewers. The search may require several iterations, until a proper number of reviewers who agree to review the paper is found (normally three). The reviewers also negotiate with the editor a deadline for returning their evaluation, to which they are expected to commit.[4] Reviewers' reports are expected to provide a detailed dissection of the paper, with constructive suggestions to the authors on how to improve it. They are also expected to provide a recommendation, which may be: accept for publication, reject, or (most likely) revise for further review. Based on the reports and the recommendations of individual reviewers, the editor (often together with the editor-in-chief) makes a final decision.

---

[3]Conflict of interests is discussed at length in Chap. 6.

[4]Unfortunately, reality shows that often these deadlines are not respected.

Revisions can be of two kinds: *major* or *minor*. In the former case, a second iteration of the review process is started upon resubmission, followed by a final decision. In the latter case, the revised paper requires a less extensive revision, and the review can consist of a simple check that the authors implemented the requested changes properly. This check may be done directly by the editor-in-chief or by a delegated editor.

Let us now consider peer-reviewed conferences. The process I describe here applies with small variations to most conferences. A conference has a *program committee*, which is responsible for the technical program. The committee is chaired by one or more *program co-chairs*. Members of the program committee are responsible for reviewing papers. Each paper is reviewed, typically by three members, and there is a hard deadline within which all reviews must be collected. The decision about the papers to accept for presentation at the conference and publication in the conference proceedings is collectively made in a meeting by all members of the program committee. When each paper is discussed, the original

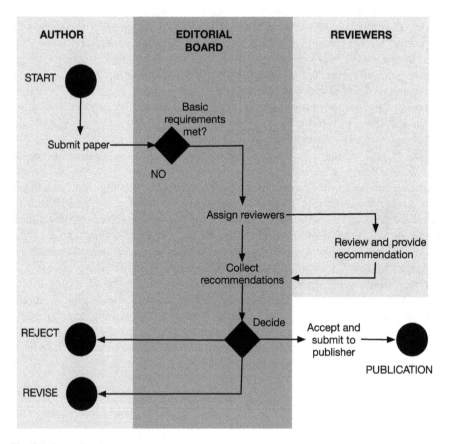

Fig. 3.1 Journal review process

reviewers play a major role in achieving a final decision. The meeting can be done face-to-face or remotely, through computer-supported conference management tools.

This simple structure works for small conferences. It hardly scales to larger conferences, which may attract hundreds, or even thousands, of submissions. Larger conferences may be organized in tracks, according to sub-topics, and have separate sub-committees per track. Or they may be structured hierarchically in terms of a large program committee, whose members act as reviewers, and a smaller-size program board, which collectively decides about acceptance based on the reviews. The principles of fair reviewing and avoidance of conflict of interest apply for conferences as well. Conferences normally take a binary decision about submissions (accept/reject), because they cannot accommodate long revision processes. They have a fixed decision date.[5] An interesting (and controversial) point concerns *anonymity* in the peer-review process. Reviewers are generally undisclosed to authors, while authors are known to the reviewers. This setting is called *single-blind* review, and it is meant to allow reviewers to be frank in expressing their opinions, shielding them from potential intimidation. Consider, for example, the case of a young researcher who is asked to review a paper from a well-known and politically influential senior researcher, who may later be involved in crucial decisions regarding his career, such as promotion or research funding. The young researcher might feel uncomfortable in giving a negative review of the paper by the senior researcher. Single-blind reviews may also raise fairness problems, which generate counterargument to anonymity of reviewers. Being shielded by anonymity, reviewers may in fact act irresponsibly or even unethically.

A *double-blind* review process is also possible, and became increasingly adopted in the recent years. In this case, not only the reviewers are undisclosed to the authors, but also the authors are undisclosed to the reviewers. The goal is to prevent a reviewer's decision based on the authors instead of the contents. Reviewers might in fact reduce their level of scrutiny for papers authored by well-known researchers, or they might have negative misconceptions about papers authored by researchers from secondary institutions. To allow double-blind review, the authors must remove from the paper any possible information that might lead to revealing their identity. This may sometimes be awkward, especially when referring to the author's previous work.

More recently, a completely different approach has also emerged, called *open peer-review*. In this process, which is part of the broader *open-science* movement discussed next in Sect. 3.7, the identity of the reviewers of papers submitted to a journal or a conference are disclosed to the authors. The entire pre-publication process of the article is posted in a public repository, not only the signed reviews, but also the history of revisions of the paper and author responses to the reviewers. This makes the review process an open and social process. This approach is meant to

---

[5]In some cases, papers may be conditionally accepted, subject to certain modifications to be made in the final manuscript.

overcome the pitfalls of traditional blind review processes. Specifically, it is meant to foster reviewers' accountability and quality of reviews. Reviewers may be rewarded for their work and this further incentivizes quality. Public evidence of excellence in reviewing is indeed a valuable contribution to research that should be considered in hiring and promotion cases. Open peer-review is still in its infancy and it needs to be understood more before it can be considered as a possible replacement for more established processes. In particular, the issue of shielding young reviewers from possible intimidation by senior authors remains open.

3.5   The Publication World

We have seen that researchers are the main actors in the scientific publication world. Not only they produce the material for publication, but they also help to select what is published and improve its contents. Researchers, however, are not the only ones. Who are the other actors involved in the publication process? And since publications are made available worldwide, how is the process regulated on a global scale? These are the issues we discuss in this section.

The publication world obeys to international standards, which ensure that all publications can be uniquely referenced. This became crucial since the publications became referenceable, retrievable, and available in digital form. Books are uniquely identified by their *International Standard Book Number* (ISBN). The ISBN is 13 digits long and is assigned to each edition of a book. A *Digital Object Identifier* (DOI) is mainly used for research outputs, such as journal articles, research reports and data sets, and even other types of information, such as videos. A DOI may be automatically resolved to access the digital object to which it refers. The *Open Researcher and Contributor ID* (ORCID) is a persistent digital identifier that uniquely identifies a researcher. It has been introduced to support integration in key research workflows such as manuscript and grant submission and supports automated linkages between a researcher and his professional activities and outputs.

A unique role in promoting research in society and publication of research products is played by *professional societies*. Professional societies exist at international and national levels in all fields. In our context, they group and represent researchers working in specific scientific fields. For example, the American Physical Society (APS) and the European Physical Society (EPS) are non-profit organizations representing researchers in Physics. The IEEE (Institute of Electrical and Electronics Engineers) is the world's largest technical professional organization for the advancement of technology. It includes societies for professionals and researchers in technological fields, from Aerospace to Circuits and Systems, Computers, Control Systems, Intelligent Transportation Systems, Photonics, and many others. The Association for Computing Machinery (ACM) is the main professional and academic organization for Informatics. Societies are largely self-managed by professionals and researchers, who run their scientific activities as a service to the community. They also provide their own support staff. Their activities are sustained by their membership fees and by the revenues from their support activities, which include publications and conference organization.

Societies run both scientific journals and conferences. For example, among many others, the APS publishes Physical Review Letters, the IEEE publishes the Transactions on Computers and the Transactions on Software Engineering, the ACM publishes Journal of the ACM, Communications of the ACM, Transactions on Programming Languages and Systems. Besides journals, societies support research dissemination through scientific conferences. Societies also support a research field by recognizing the exceptional contributions of their members through awards. Certain awards are extremely prestigious. For example, the ACM Turing Award is an annual prize given to an individual selected for contributions "of lasting and major technical importance to the computer field." This award is generally recognized as the highest distinction in Informatics (the "Nobel Prize of Informatics").

Commercial publishers, such as Springer, Wiley, or Elsevier, also play a very important role in scientific publications. Besides educational books, they publish research monographs, conference proceedings, and scientific journals. Even in these cases, researchers lead the scientific strategy and have editorial responsibility in the reviewing and selection of the published material. Academic institutions may also have their own publishing organization. For example, the MIT Press is a university press affiliated with the Massachusetts Institute of Technology. It is a publisher of books and journals whose editorial board consists of MIT faculty members.

Researchers have plenty of choices for the venues where their research results may be published. There are journals and conferences which aim at broad coverage of a field, while others are more narrowly focused. Some set the bar for acceptance very high, while others are less selective. Some venues are highly valued by a particular research community, and publishing in these venues is regarded as a sign of distinction. Beginning researchers may be disoriented when they have to choose among the many opportunities that are offered to them. They should ask for advice to their advisors or other senior researchers to identify valid publication targets with a good reputation. It is important for them to learn how to navigate safely in the publication world. The world has recently become more like a jungle, due to the continuous proliferation of new publishers and new venues. New venues can be justified by the need to offer a home to new emerging research areas. More often, proliferation is hardly justifiable, and only serves the purpose of offering easy options to researchers who are willing to trade quantity over quality in their scientific production. The jungle, as I mentioned in Sect. 3.2, is also inhabited by predatory publishers, which should be carefully spotted and avoided, since they damage the reputation of the scientific dissemination process.

3.6   Other Forms of Dissemination

Publications are the primary and most traditional vehicles to disseminate research results. Other forms have also been emerging in the past decades, mainly thanks

> **Box 3.3: Sharing a Research Artifact: An Example**
>
> An Informatics researcher (John) has been working on a new static program analysis technique to detect software errors. John has published a paper illustrating the theory behind his method, which applies to the specific constructs offered by programming language L. He has validated the approach by building a prototype analyzer $P1$, and by using it to analyze existing programs. Experimental results demonstrate the potential benefits of the new technique. Another researcher (Ann), after reading the paper presented by John on his static analysis technique at the recent International Conference on Software Engineering, has a brilliant idea to extend and improve the method. She develops the theory underlying her idea and then she needs to proceed to validation, to show its benefits through experiments. Since she does not have access to the prototype developed by John, she needs to build her new prototype $P2$ from scratch. $P2$, however, might be more easily built starting from $P1$, since the changes implied by the new algorithms invented by Ann are confined to well-defined parts of $P1$'s architecture. The ability to access $P1$ and modify it to produce $P2$ would save Ann a lot of time.

to digital technologies, which support diffusion of a variety of additional artifacts beyond text. In general, these should not be viewed as substitutes for scientific papers, but rather as complements and enrichments. Examples are: data sets, videos, simulations, software tools, and any kinds of software demonstrators. These additional forms of dissemination are very important in experimental research, where experimental data can be shared with other researchers to reproduce experiments. There is a consensus that an experimental result is not fully established unless it can be independently reproduced. It still happens, unfortunately, that a large number of research results found in the literature fail this test, because of sloppy experimental methods, flawed statistical analyses, or even fraud. By sharing their experimental data, researchers can facilitate the set-up of additional experimental campaigns, which may lead to comparisons, may reinforce validity of findings, and possibly generate new findings.

Dissemination of artifacts plays an even more fundamental role in constructive research, whose goal is indeed development of concrete artifacts. If the artifact is a software tool or a simulation package, it can be stored, transferred, or even remotely accessed by others, who can access and use the artifact, not just its published description. Hereafter I focus on artifacts in digital form.

Artifact sharing can bring tremendous benefits to research development. By accessing the artifacts produced by others, new research can more effectively build on previous research and its progress can be faster, as discussed through an example in Box 3.3.

In reality, effective artifact sharing is easier said than done, and in practice both reuse of experimental data and of research prototype implementations described in scientific paper are still poorly supported. When a paper is submitted, there is no mandatory requirement that the associated artifacts upon which the paper is based should also be submitted, and when the paper is reviewed, the associated artifacts are seldom reviewed or even examined by reviewers. For this reason, researchers don't feel an obligation to invest much of their time in developing artifacts, because this may distract them from other activities they consider more rewarding. When a researcher develops an artifact to support validation of a research finding, it is often done for personal use, and not meant to be usable also by others. On the other hand, since papers often refer to artifacts and claim certain properties about them, they raise expectations that are not subject to any formal review and may not stand against attempts by other researchers to build on them.

In the case of analytic research, consider a paper reporting experimental data that support a certain theory. What should be shared and which are the quality requirements for effective sharing of the data? In the case of constructive research, consider a paper presenting a new artifact and describing experiments in which the artifact has been successfully used. What makes the artifact suitable and ready for dissemination? The terminology in use in this context is not uniform. Hereafter I refer to the terminology adopted by the ACM [1], reported hereafter with minor changes.

For an experiment, we may consider the following qualities:

- *Repeatability* (Same team, same experimental setup). The results of the reported experiments can be obtained with stated precision by the same team using the same experimental setup, under the same operating conditions, in the same location on multiple trials. Repeatability is the minimum, bottom-line prerequisite for dissemination of a research result.
- *Replicability* (Different team, same experimental setup). The results of the reported experiments can be obtained with stated precision by a different team using the same experimental setup, under the same operating conditions, in the same or a different location on multiple trials. If experiments concern the use of an artifact, which is the main subject of a paper, replicability means that the experiments reported in the paper and all the use cases described for the artifact can be re-checked. A check would require re-running a bundled software made available by the authors on the cases presented in the paper. For example, replicability ensures that the data set used to validate a new sophisticated algorithm described in a paper can be re-run and produces the same results under absolutely identical execution conditions.
- *Reproducibility* (Different team, different experimental setup). This results of the reported experiment can be obtained with stated precision by a different team, a different experimental setup, in a different location on multiple trials. For computational experiments, this means that an independent group can obtain the same result using artifacts which they develop completely independently.

Although reproducibility might be considered as the ultimate goal, replicability is a significant intermediate step and we should promote practices that can ensure replicability. To promote both the integrity of research and improve research dissemination, there are attempts to include a kind of auditing process for artifacts as part of the reviewing process. The ACM has been encouraging this practice in the field of Informatics and has defined specific policies for artifact reviewing (see Box 3.4). As a result of the review, papers are labeled, using so-called *badges*, to indicate the kind of artifact review associated with it. The policy recommends that three separate labels should be used: *artifact evaluated* (AE), *artifact available* (AA), and *results validated* (RV). The badges are considered independent and any one, two, or all three can be applied to any paper depending on review procedures developed by the journal or conference.

Artifact evaluation can be given as an option to authors when they submit a paper. If the paper is accepted, authors may submit the associated artifact for review. Reviewers check it against the possible qualities and officially label the paper in the journal or conference proceedings withe the corresponding badges. Badges are a kind of distinction for validated artifact papers and give them a higher status among published unlabeled papers.

The on-going discussion and current efforts on artifact dissemination may be viewed as a step in a direction that takes a holistic view of what is a research product This view encompasses a paper describing the findings and all its support artifacts. The ultimate goal is making diffusion of research results more effective and facilitate the progress of research. Since research progress may highly benefit from the diffusion of artifacts, why didn't artifact review become a standard practice? Why hasn't artifact review been experimented earlier by journals and conferences as part of the peer review process? The first reason is that the possibility to share artifacts has only become realistic on a large scale through the recent digital transformation, which is profoundly changing the traditional scientific process. We can only realistically consider review and dissemination for digital, rather than physical, artifacts. The second is that publishers or other reliable entities should also be responsible for keeping and maintaining artifacts, and not only papers, in digital libraries. Third, promoting artifacts to a first-class publication status requires a cultural change. This is no surprise. Social processes are subject to inertia, and possible changes may take time to become reality. The research community should incentivize artifact sharing among researchers, and researchers should be rewarded according to the impact of their research on others. Publishing papers is a way to disseminate research results and possibly generate impact, but impact is amplified if the associated artifacts also become public and undergo the same level of careful scrutiny before they are disseminated and are used by other researchers. There are of course exceptions, as in the case of research done under a contract where a non-disclosure agreement prevents artifact dissemination.

Box 3.4: ACM Artifact Sharing Policy

The ACM has published a policy [1] to "promote the integrity of the research ecosystem by developing review processes that increase the likelihood that results can be independently replicated and reproduced." The policy recommends that three separate *badges* related to artifact review be associated with publications: *artifact evaluated* (AE), *artifact available* (AA), and *results validated* (RV). AE can be of two kinds: *artifact evaluated functional* (AEF) or *artifact evaluated reusable* (AER). AEF indicates that "the artifacts associated with the research are found to be documented, consistent, complete, exercisable, and include appropriate evidence of verification and validation." AER indicates that "the artifacts associated with the paper are of a quality that significantly exceeds minimal functionality. That is, they have all the qualities of the Artifacts Evaluated - Functional level, but, in addition, they are very carefully documented and well-structured to the extent that reuse and repurposing is facilitated. In particular, norms and standards of the research community for artifacts of this type are strictly adhered to." Box 3.3 presents an example where reusability would be desirable.

AA indicates that "Author-created artifacts relevant to this paper have been placed on a publicly accessible archival repository. A DOI or link to this repository along with a unique identifier for the object is provided."

RV indicates that "the main results of the paper have been successfully obtained by a person or team other than the author." Result validation can be of two kinds: *replication* (*Repl*) or *reproduction* (*Repr*). The *Repl* badge is assigned if "the main results of the paper have been obtained in a subsequent study by a person or team other than the authors, using, in part, artifacts provided by the author." The *Repr* badge is assigned if "the main results of the paper have been independently obtained in a subsequent study by a person or team other than the authors, without the use of author-supplied artifacts."

A research paper that develop an algorithm or describes a software system could be labeled as *Repl*. Here, the artifacts could be an implementation of the algorithm or complete software system, and replication would involve exercise of software provided by the author. Likewise, consider a paper reporting human-subject studies of novel human-computer interface modalities. The associated artifacts might be the collected data, as well as the scripts developed to analyze the data. Replication might focus on a careful inspection of the experimental protocol along with independent analysis of the collected data.

3.7   Towards Open Science

This section presents the on-going debate on *open science*, which is driving change in how research results are disseminated. The term "open science" indicates that no barriers should hinder diffusion of publications and the associated artifacts. To better understand the motivations that drive this evolution, let us step back and revisit the context in which the traditional publication process is embedded.

Research is mainly supported by public investments, through grants, researcher salaries, and scholarships for students and fresh graduates. Researchers are not remunerated for spreading research results: it is one of their duties, and their return is in terms of knowledge, recognition, and prestige. They produce intellectual products, which are subject to regulations on the protection of intellectual property. Copyright is a way to protect publications, ensuring that authors receive recognition for their work.[6] In the traditional publication process, authors transfer copyright for their publications to the publishers. This is often justified by the claim that publishers can do a better job than authors of protecting their rights, ensuring proper use, and coordinating permissions for reprints. Publishers sustain the costs of advertising publications, managing the editorial process, printing and distribution, and electronic archiving. Researchers further sustain the publication process by providing voluntary unpaid support to reviewing papers. Research institutions, as well as individual researchers, must pay a subscription fee to access published material. An institution does that also for its own financed research. Subscription fees, which may include access to digital libraries, are substantial. This can be a serious problem, since research institutions increasingly face budget cuts and have to deal with cost reduction problems.

The traditional approach to disseminating science has evident problems and generated critical reactions from researchers. The possibility of changing publication policies towards more open access to research products has been triggered by the progress in digitalization that occurred since the 1990s. The web has made it possible to post and share papers online, eliminating printing costs, making distribution instantaneous, unlimited, with no borders, and potentially free. Readers can access and download any research result without barriers.

arXiv has been the first example of an online public repository of scientific papers. It was created in 1991, and it is owned and operated by Cornell University as a non-profit institution. It immediately became extremely successful as an example of an effective cyber-space in which researchers may freely share their published contributions. Successful progress in electronic archiving ignited a movement among researchers, who voiced their objection to the traditional way of managing and regulating access to knowledge, which remained locked behind technical, legal, financial barriers. Technological progress showed that immediate knowledge sharing is possible: everybody can create new knowledge and share it,

---

[6]Patents may also be generated to protect a researcher's invention. I provide comments on patents later in this section.

and everybody can access it without restrictions. This generated the trend towards open access, as an alternative way to publish research results. The unrestricted on-line distribution of research material meets the demand from authors (whose work gets seen by more people), readers (who can access the most recent work in the field), and funders (as the work they fund becomes more widely visible and potentially has broader impact).

Let us look more closely to the ground principles of open access. What makes a work product open access? It must satisfy four requirements:

1. It must be available in digital form.
2. It must be available on-line.
3. It must be free of charge (also called *gratis*).
4. It must be free of most copyright and licensing restrictions (also called *libre*).

There are two ways of implementing the open access principles to publications: gold and green open access. *Gold open access* is the purest form of open access publication. It makes the final version of an article freely and permanently accessible for everyone, immediately after publication. Copyright for the article is retained by the authors and most of the permission barriers are removed. Gold open access articles can be published either in fully open access journals (where all the content is published open access) or hybrid journals (a subscription-based journal that offers an open access option which authors can chose if they wish). To make the process economically viable, publishers often ask authors to pay a publication fee.[7] Authors can pay the fees using their research funding, if this is permitted by the research funding body. There are also cases where the costs of open access publishing are covered by subsidies or other funding models.[8] *Green open access* instead means that the author can self-archive a version of the published and reviewed paper in an open access repository (such as arXiv). The version that can be deposited into a repository (for example, pre-print or authors' post-print) depends on the publisher. In summary, the author can:

- Publish the paper in a traditional journal.
- Deposit a suitable version in a public repository. Depositors are responsible for obtaining the needed rights or permissions on their own.
- Define the conditions under which the paper may be accessed, in accordance with the original publisher, which may impose an initial *embargo period*.
- Define additional use conditions based on own retained rights.[9]

---

[7]Fees vary a lot depending on the publisher and on the journal. For example, the publishing fees of a well-known publisher range from US$ 150 to US$ 6000.

[8]The term *platinum open access* is sometimes used to refer to gold open access journals that do not charge any author fees. They are usually financed by a university or research organization.

[9]Unlike Gold open access, the copyright for these papers is usually owned by the publisher and there are restrictions as to how the work can be reused.

> ## Box 3.5: An Example Copyright Policy
>
> As an example of a copyright policy, hereafter I quote from the ACM's publication policies[10]:
>
> > ACM requires authors to assign publication rights to ACM as a condition of publishing the work. ACM relies on either an assignment of copyright with permanent rights reserved to the author, or an equivalent grant of a license. ACM treats the rights granted as the basic means of obtaining certain exclusive publication rights; to create and deliver the Digital Library; to further disseminate works by acting as a single source for blanket republication requests, such as aggregated collections or translations, and the delivery of the material to the requesting party; to protect works from plagiarism and any other unauthorized uses; and to sustain and develop its publishing program by selling subscriptions or charging for access to its collections.
> > . . .
> >
> > The original Owner/Author permanently holds these rights:
> >
> > - All other proprietary rights not granted to ACM, including patent or trademark rights.
> > - Reuse of any portion of the Work, without fee, in any future works written or edited by the Author, including books, lectures and presentations in any and all media.
> > - Create a "Major Revision" which is not subject to any rights in the original that have been granted to ACM
> > - Post the Accepted Version of the Work on (1) the Author's home page, (2) the Owner's institutional repository, (3) any repository legally mandated by an agency funding the research on which the Work is based, and (4) any non-commercial repository or aggregation that does not duplicate ACM tables of contents, i.e., whose patterns of links do not substantially duplicate an ACM-copyrighted volume or issue. Non-commercial repositories are here understood as repositories owned by non-profit organizations that do not charge a fee for accessing deposited articles and that do not sell advertising or otherwise profit from serving articles.
> >
> > . . .
> >
> > ACM grants gratis permission for individual digital or hard copies made without fee for use in academic classrooms and for use by individuals in personal research and study. Further reproduction or distribution requires explicit permission and possibly a fee.

Open access has generated changes in the business models of publishers, who came from the traditional publication process and evolved towards offering different kinds of publishing options, which includes open access. Box 3.5 describes an example of an existing policy by a traditional publisher.

The openness principles we discussed so far for papers hold for other artifacts as well. The notion of *open data* applies to datasets. This means that the data produced

---

[10]The full text may be found here https://www.acm.org/publications/policies/copyright-policy.

by the research should be freely available to everyone to use and republish as they wish, without restrictions from copyright, patents or other mechanisms of control. Likewise, if the artifact is a piece of software, the principle of openness applies to software as well. A software is libre if it is accessible to any potential users through some kinds of permissive licenses, for example Creative Commons. In other terms, authors retain *some rights* rather than *all rights*. These are examples of licenses:

- CC Zero. This license assigns the work to the public domain. The author waives all rights, including those of attribution of the work to oneself.
- CC BY. This license allows any use, provided the user attributes the work to the original author.
- CC BY-SA. This license allows others to remix, tweak, and build upon the work even for commercial purposes, as long as they credit the author and license their new creations under the identical terms.

The software is defined to be *open source* if its source code is released under a license in which the copyright holder grants users the rights to study, change, and distribute the software to anyone and for any purpose.

The principles of open science also inform other aspects of research diffusion, such as Open Peer Review, which was mentioned in Sect. 3.4.

3.8 Conclusions

Researchers are heavily involved both in the development of research and in the dissemination of its results. These are two equally important aspects of their work: research often has no value until it goes public. Researchers spend their efforts in diffusing their own research and also in supporting the dissemination efforts of other researchers. A huge cooperative worldwide network connecting researchers has been active even before the Internet was invented to support the global research processes. This is the network through which researchers have been able to sustain and self-manage the progress of research. Scientists tried to find ways to network even in dark times when politics erected walls to separate nations, like during the cold war.

There is an intrinsic aspiration in research towards openness and sharing. Diffusion is at the heart of research. There are also cases where research is privately funded and research results are proprietary. Their public disclosure may be forbidden, or it may be severely limited. By and large, however, research is a public, open, and social process, whose results are for the benefit of society. It is no surprise that researchers are currently engaged in a debate on how the publication world should evolve, as in the case of discussion on open access. Exploration of possible evolution paths is valuable, but it should preserve and possibly even strengthen the main values targeted by traditional research dissemination: integrity and severity of reviewing, and promotion of quality.

As a final remark, it is important to stress that this chapter has focused on research dissemination through scientific channels. Other forms of dissemination are also possible to reach out a broader audience and even the general public. As I mentioned before, engaging with society in communicating research results and in discussing their potential effects is becoming increasingly relevant for researchers. This can be achieved through a variety of means, including participation in public debates, videos, blogs, articles, and so on.

3.9 Further Reading

Writing is a fundamental skill that should be mastered by researchers. It is essential to disseminate research results. A reader interested in learning more about writing style in general should refer to the classic [55]. For technical writing I strongly recommend referring to Ramsey's on-line material [45]; Zobel's book [67] is an excellent reference for technical writing in Computer Science.

For an excellent discussion of the issues involved in artifact dissemination, the reader may refer to [29].

To go deeper into open access, one may refer to [56]. It is also interesting to understand how open access may be enforced by research policies. The EU has adopted the principles of open access in its funding program called Horizon 2020 and has issued an interesting document "Guidelines to the Rules on Open Access to Scientific Publications and Open Access to Research Data" [47].

Chapter 4
The Researcher's Progress

This chapter focuses on how researchers progress in their career. The presentation actually starts one step earlier, before one decides to engage in research, and even before one considers research as a possible professional option for the future. I present how one can move through a doctoral study, through the subsequent steps as a post-doc, and how one can then progress towards becoming an independent researcher. I mainly focus on research in academic institutions, although similar considerations may apply also to progress in public research laboratories, or—to a lesser extent—in industry. The main goal is to help potential future researchers and junior researchers to understand the world of research. Hopefully, this may enable them to be prepared for the main challenges they have to face and successfully overcome them. Senior researchers may also find in this chapter some possible food for thought for their student supervision activities and mentoring of junior colleagues.

As for any personal progress through life, the researcher's progress is not linear and one should feel free at any time to change direction, including the decision to leave research and move professionally in other sectors. Every individual should try to realize her potentials in the best possible way, and possible changes of direction should never be viewed as failures, but rather as moves towards better personal opportunities and self-accomplishment.

This chapter is organized as follows. In Sect. 4.1 I try to identify what makes a young person a prospective researcher. In Sects. 4.2 and 4.3 I discuss the main options one should evaluate to enter a PhD program and the skills one should acquire. Section 4.4 focuses on the progress towards becoming a successful independent researcher. Section 4.5 provides some conclusive remarks on why one should consider becoming a researcher.

© Springer Nature Switzerland AG 2020
C. Ghezzi, *Being a Researcher*, https://doi.org/10.1007/978-3-030-45157-8_4

4.1   Am I Fit for Research?

Young people meet research for the first time when they are studying for their Bachelor degree. They get in touch with it through their professors, who often are active researchers. Sometimes students are lucky to meet professors who are enthusiastic about their work, share their passion, and try to instill an interest in research into them while they teach a course. Sometimes professors offer opportunities to students to participate in their own research, for example through internships. Sometimes the opportunity is offered through a project, a Bachelor, or a Master thesis.

Academic institutions should put their best efforts into offering students a variety of opportunities to raise their potential interest in research. In fact, most young people often have no idea of what research is all about and even ignore that becoming a researcher can be an option for their professional life. Being personally engaged in doing research—"in vivo", e.g. through a project or an internship—is the best way for them to understand what it means to do research, whether one feels an interest in it, and whether one feels fit for it. Often students even have misconceptions about research. They view research as an esoteric activity and researchers as obsessed individuals, disconnected from reality, and locked into their own private ivory tower. By engaging personally with research they may realize how stereotypical this view is. Researchers can be very social persons with lots of interests and a real passion for their work. Students may realize that research is challenging and fun, and can provide a deep sense of intellectual fulfillment. They may realize that it is a world open to diversity and cooperation.

The question whether one is fit for research merits some further discussion. Quite naturally, people ask themselves whether they are fit before they may start engaging in any activity. This is true for research too. Senior researchers may also ask the same question when they announce an open research position and then they have to select the best candidate among applicants.

A candidate's track record as a student is often the only relevant piece of available information to guide a decision. Unfortunately, it is not a reliable piece of information. Being an excellent student with excellent grades does not necessarily indicate that one is fit for research. A mediocre student may turn out to be an extremely talented researcher.[1] During my long life in research, I have met both students with an outstanding track record who did not prove to be fit for research and students with a mediocre track record who bloomed as researchers.

This is a personal, partial list of key abilities I consider as possible indicators for being fit for research:

- intellectual curiosity;
- openness to new ideas;
- willingness to learn more;

---

[1]Einstein described himself as a mediocre student [53].

- attraction to engaging with non-trivial problems;
- persistence in problem solving;
- ability to critically assess and go beyond the apparently obvious answers;
- rigor;
- ambition;
- resilience to failure;
- ability to abstract and formalize;
- analytical skills;
- mathematical skills;
- ability to collaborate.

In an attempt to exemplify what characterizes a potential researcher, and in particular as an example of what "ability to critically assess and go beyond the apparently obvious answers" means, in his thoughtful book "Advice to a Young Scientist", Peter Medawar [34] suggests a test in logic through which one is challenged to explain a striking feature of the paintings by the famous artist El Greco (1541–1614). El Greco's figures and faces often look oddly stretched, as for example in his painting of Saint Jerome as scholar shown in Fig. 4.1.

In trying to explain El Greco's distinctive feature—an apparently awkward style—an ophthalmologist proposed that the painter suffered from a form of astigmatism, which distorted his vision and led him to see people this way. Although such an explanation may initially seem reasonable, it "does not go beyond the apparently obvious answer", and does not stand up to logical scrutiny. Critical assessment and analytic reasoning come to help. Suppose, in fact, that El Greco did see the world through a distorting lens. The same distortion would apply to what he saw on his canvas! The only rationally plausible explanation is that figures appear so because this was El Greco's intention.

I would like to stress another important ability mentioned in my personal list: the ability to collaborate. Contemporary research is seldom done in isolation. A researcher must be able to collaborate with the students she supervises or mentors. She must be able to collaborate with colleagues or with industrial partners on joint research projects. A researcher is part of a research community within which research results are shared. She collaborates also by providing service, for example as a peer reviewer. To conclude, a broad set of abilities contribute to defining what it means to be fit for research. These abilities, however, are hard to assess a-priori. They can only be tested as one engages in a research activity. If a student has an interest in research and thinks she can do it, she should try to find an opportunity to try it out. The student can then strengthen or even develop her skills by enrolling in a doctoral program, where she is educated for a career as a researcher. I discuss doctoral education in the next section.

4.2 Entering a Doctoral Program

Once a young person decides to engage in research, what are the important decisions to make? What are the essential skills one should acquire and master? These are the questions we address in this and in the next section. A Doctor of Philosophy (PhD) program is dedicated to educating researchers. Today, a PhD degree is universally considered as the main entrance door into, and a prerequisite for, a research career. Thus the first questions the young person has to ask himself is *when* he should do this, *where* he should apply for admission, and *how* should he choose a research topic and an advisor who follows him throughout his adventure.

As for the first question, one should comply with the existing admission requirements. In most Anglo-Saxon countries, admission in a PhD program is possible for students who have a Bachelor degree; most universities of continental Europe instead require a Master degree. In many cases, students move on to PhD directly from their Bachelor or Master, but there are also cases where one decides to go back to school for a doctoral degree, for example after a period of work in industry.

Deciding where to apply is a crucial decision. Often one comes from an experience in research during her Bachelor or Master, for example an internship or a thesis. Often the senior researcher she was working with suggests continuing with a PhD, staying in the same department. This may be an opportunity to consider, but it may be wise to look around for other opportunities in other academic institutions before deciding. If the student has already made a choice of the area in which she wants to work, she may look for openings in departments that have a strong research presence in the area of interest. Prestige of the department, opportunities offered to students, location, and personal considerations normally guide a decision.

I would like to offer a potential applicant a few words of advice regarding this initial important decision. First, choose a reputable department where you can see active research happening that has aroused your enthusiasm, admiration, or respect. Don't just decide to go for the first place that makes you an offer. Second, look for departments with a lively scientific atmosphere, which foster collaborations, and where you do not work in complete isolation. Isolation is disagreeable and almost always bad. The opportunity to open your eyes beyond your main research topic, which absorbs most of your time, enriches you and amplifies your mindset.

The most crucial, related decisions concern the choice of the research topic and of the advisor. They are crucial decisions because students work with their advisor and on a certain topic for a number of years. Success of the PhD adventure depends heavily on these decisions. The way these decisions are made may vary across different academic systems in different countries. In some cases, once admitted in the PhD program, a student has some time to look around before committing to a topic and advisor. In other cases, the choice occurs even before admission: a PhD candidate establishes a direct connection with a potential advisor and applies for admission only after the advisor accepts to work with him. In other cases, the choice of the advisor occurs soon afterwards, through bilateral conversations and mutual agreement.

Let us focus first on the choice of an advisor. A *doctoral advisor* (also called *supervisor*) is a faculty member of the department whose role is to guide a PhD candidate, helping him with her advice, throughout the process he has to follow in his graduate work. A PhD candidate is normally required to take several graduate courses (although there are also PhD programs with very limited course requirements). He may be involved in teaching activities. Most important: he has to choose a research area and a specific topic for his research and for the final dissertation. The advisor is expected to give her advice on these crucial decisions. The advisor works closely with the PhD candidate throughout the research: she monitors progress, suggests changes to its direction, collaborates in disseminating results, and in the end decides when the candidate matured enough research results that warrant writing and then discussing a dissertation. Finally, the advisor may be a member of the final doctoral examination committee, which grants the PhD degree. Different academic systems, however, may differ quite substantially in the way dissertations are evaluated and approved, in the composition of the evaluation committee, in the way the final step of the process is handled, and in the role the advisor plays in them. It would be impossible here to list all possible variations. Needless to say, a PhD candidate must be fully aware of the organization of the program he is enrolled in.

Students generally choose an advisor based on their interest in her research within a broader discipline, on their respect for her, and on their desire to work closely with her. The advisor almost inevitably plays a role model for the PhD student. On the other side, the potential advisor must be available and interested in working with the student. When a student identifies a potential advisor, he should keep in mind that research has a pretty large component of *learning by apprenticeship*: a lot of knowledge, both about the specific research field and about research in general gradually and mostly informally emerges in the relationship with the advisor. Personal interaction and good feeling with the advisor are key. One can probably say that the choice of the advisor is at least as important of the choice of the main research topic.

The interpersonal chemistry of the relationship between PhD students and advisors depends on many factors, which are to be ascribed to their individual personalities. In our context, we focus the discussion on personality traits that are relevant in research interpersonal relationships. Box 4.1 briefly illustrates the variety of researchers' personalities. Most important, a student choosing an advisor should consider that advisors have both different personalities and different relational styles. Before committing, a PhD candidate should try to get as much information as possible about the advisor, not only by looking at her past record, but also trying to get direct, first-hand information, for example talking to other students. To guide the decision, a PhD candidate should ask himself several questions, such as:

- How much direction/independence do I want? Some advisors tend to offer a well-defined and thesis-scoped problem to work on; others have a more open style and ask the candidate to explore an area and come out with a research proposal.
- How much contact do I want? Some advisors meet students often and regularly (e.g, on a weekly basis) for progress reports; others don't, and expect the student to take the initiative when they feel it necessary.
- What style of interaction am I interested in? Some advisors view their role as "senior co-workers"; others give students full responsibility and independence, and only provide inputs to steer their progress.
- Is the advisor scientifically well connected? Scientific connections within the research community (both national and international) are a sign of visibility and are important for the candidate to look outside his home institution and establish his own networking.
- How much pressure do I want? Some advisors set strong requirements in terms of publication they expect the candidate to produce and very much work with deadlines. Others have a more relaxed approach.
- How much personal support do I want? Do I want to establish a relation that only concerns technical work, or am I also interested in a broader relation, e.g. covering cultural and personal aspects?
- What kind of research group/environment does the advisor provide? Some advisors only have one or two students, working in isolation on disjoint problems. Some have larger groups, working on a set of related problems in a broad research area. Some have external collaborations with industry, or engage in large multi-site research projects.
- Is financial support available? Is it adequate? Does the financial support require certain obligations on my side?

Let me provide now a few words of advice regarding the choice of the research topic. This is crucial decision, regarding a unique opportunity, which probably

Box 4.1: Researchers' Personalities

All individuals, including researchers, have different personalities. It may be interesting to try to characterize the main kinds with respect to research. This may help to realize what is kind of researcher one is, either to exploit and cultivate it, or to forge it.

I. Berlin, in a famous essay [4], classifies writers and thinkers into two categories: hedgehogs and wolfs. The distinction alludes to a fragment attributed to the Greek poet Archilochus, which says: "The fox knows many things, but the hedgehog knows one big thing." In Berlin's words:

> (*hedgehogs*) relate everything to a single central vision, one system, less or more coherent or articulate, in terms of which they understand, think and feel—a single organising principle in terms of which alone all that they are and say has significance—and, on the other side (*foxes are*) those who pursue many ends, often unrelated and even contradictory, connected, if at all, only in some de facto way...

Researchers can also be either foxes or hedgehogs. They can excel by switching to different topics and adopting different approaches, or they just interested and excel in a specific area.

P.B. Medawar [33] provides a finer-grain characterization of different research personalities:

> Scientists are people of very dissimilar temperaments doing different things in very different ways. Among scientists are collectors, classifiers, and compulsive tidiers-up; many are detectives by temperament and many are explorers; some are artists and other are artisans. There are poet-scientists and philosopher-scientists and even a few mystics.What sort of mind or temperament can all these people be supposed to have in common? Obligative scientists must be very rare, and most people who are in fact scientists could easily have been something else instead.

A further characterization is proposed by Gosling and Noordam [18]. Four categories are used to define personalities:

1. How one copes with the world: *extrovert versus introvert*. For example, in a meeting one may mostly act and talk, or mostly listen and reflect.
2. How one thinks: *intuition versus sensation*. For example, one may be more interested in exploring new ideas, or is more interested in systematizing and applying existing knowledge.
3. How one decides: *thinkers versus feelers*. Thinkers decide based on factual, impersonal information. Feelers take into account the impact a decision has on others.
4. How one organizes work: *chaos versus planning*. For example, one may feel comfortable, and even enjoy chaotic processes in which the final goal only becomes clear towards the end, or one can only work in the context of a carefully planned process.

A final personality dimension concerns group work. One can excel as a soloist, or may contribute most as a team member, or even as a team leader.

will never materialize again in the future, to work full time on a substantial and challenging problem. First, and most important, one must be passionate about the topic. Nothing good comes out if one doesn't feel challenged by it or has no particular interest in it. In the end, PhD candidates needs to "defend" their work work in a thesis. Second, the topic should express the candidate's personal vision and should be clearly understandable by the research community working in the area. Third, the topic should be timely and relevant; it should have intellectual depth. I would recommend not to look for low-hanging fruit and, at the same time, also to avoid targeting too risky and monolithic topics. Ideally, the topic should be scoped in a way that makes it possible to break down the work into steps, which may lead to contributions that make sense individually and can be published separately. An incremental progress allows the candidate to get external feedback and, if needed, refocus the objectives. This leads to the fourth advice: one should realize that the topic is not carved into stone in all details when it is initially chosen, but rather it gets reshaped as one progresses. To account for this, one should keep a log of ideas as they emerge and of potential further developments. Periodically, one should revisit the existing plan, change it if needed, and prioritize the future steps as one progresses. Finally, in choosing a topic, I strongly advice to beware of the herd instinct driven by fashion. One should work on a problem only if it is relevant and interesting.

4.3 Acquiring and Mastering the Necessary Skills

After entering a PhD program, one becomes a researcher-in-training. By progressing through the program, a PhD student should

- refine his critical thinking skills,
- improve his ability to work independently and to collaborate with others,
- learn research methods and the use of research tools,
- develop oral and written presentation skills,
- understand the ethical issues involved in research,
- develop an autonomous approach to research,
- learn how to review others' work.

In this section I would like to focus in particular on five fundamental skills one should learn to master during the doctoral studies: reading, writing, presenting, building artifacts, networking.

The first fundamental skill is *reading* scientific material. Students must understand well the subject area in which their specific research is positioned and need to be aware of the state of the art of research in the specific topic they selected. They must also learn to speak the language of a research community, to become part of it. This can only be achieved by reading published work, and especially research papers. Although most reading is done in the initial stage of the research, more

---

Box 4.2: Effective Interaction with the Advisor

Regular meetings with the advisor are very important for an effective advising of PhD students. If the advisor does not adopt a structured interaction framework to interact with students, they should take the initiative, as well argued by Kearns and Gardiner [26]. It is advisable for students to schedule regular checkpoints on progress of research. Students should also be specific on the type of feedback they are looking for. They should suggest an agenda for the meeting and provide focused material to the advisor.

As observed by Kearns and Gardiner [26], the main factor affecting PhD progress is advising. Even for well accomplished scientists sometimes advising is a weaknesses. Thus PhD students need to be proactive. If the advisor is not giving the student what she needs, she needs to go out and get it. In other words: she should "ask what she needs, rather than hope that the advisor will know what to provide."

---

reading becomes necessary as one proceeds. If the topic has an interdisciplinary nature, background knowledge in other areas may also be necessary.

To be more specific, for a PhD candidate in Informatics a general background is always necessary: in theory, architecture, systems, languages, AI, and so on. A strong basic mathematical background is always key for research, but one may also need a specific in-depth inspection, for example in algebra, graph theory, logic, statistical methods, or stochastic methods, depending on the student's specific research. For interdisciplinary work, students may even need to learn about cognitive psychology, social science, philosophy, neuroscience, linguistics, control theory, or any other subject that may interface with their research. If the PhD program requires students to take courses, most of the background reading is done while taking courses.

Research-specific reading is instead both preliminary and instrumental in the course of research. A typical question a PhD student often asks is: how much more research-specific reading do I need before I can start my own work? The practical response is that one should avoid two extremes: ignoring previous work and never feeling ready. Awareness of previous work is necessary to avoid reinventing the wheel and to properly position own contributions, understanding their novelty with respect to others' contributions. Never feeling ready to start is perhaps a less common mistake, but it is a sign of immaturity and lack of self-confidence. It may be called the "Peter Pan syndrome": one fears to grow to the adult age where he is expected to provide his personal contributions. A pragmatic approach can be stated as follows:

> Start from a good understanding of the state of the art and read incrementally as you progress.

Another skill one should master is technical *writing*. Writing is an essential part of the research process. Researchers write both for themselves and for others. They write for themselves because this allows keeping track of ideas as they arise during the work. Writing also helps to clarify informal ideas and solutions and to state conjectures in precise form. Write-ups can also be used in day-by-day interactions with others: for example as background material for meetings with the advisor (see also Box 4.2). Finally, writing skills are fundamental because eventually a PhD student needs to disseminate research results through research papers and the PhD dissertation. Technical writing is different from other kinds of writing the student was familiar with before entering the PhD program: logical coherence and rigor are the key distinctive style factors that do not normally apply to other kinds of written communication. I discussed how to write scientific papers in Sect. 3.3, where I presented the basic principles and some tips. I also gave references to specialized sources of information for readers who want to go deeper into the subject of technical writing.

A third important skill is *presenting* technical work. A PhD candidate must learn to present his work, both internally in research meetings and externally. External presentations may be given in conferences or in public seminars, for example while visiting other research groups. Eventually, one almost inevitably needs to present when interviewing for a job or when applying for funding.

Technical presentations are made with the support of slides. To design a presentation, one has to understand exactly (1) the audience to which the presentation is directed and (2) the purpose of the presentation. If the presentation is private, internal to the research group or to the advisor, and the goal is to get feedback on on-going work, its tone can be informal and the contents should focus on the questions the presenter wishes to raise. If the presentation is public, and given externally to report research results to a technical audience, it should be much more carefully prepared. The next important point to consider is how much time is allocated for the presentation. This is normally a hard constraint. The amount of material that can be covered is bound by the time available. Therefore one has to decide what to cover and the level of detail, possibly trading-off depth versus breadth.

The presentation should convey a clear message about the work being reported. If the presentation is made publicly in a conference, one should consider that a paper is published in the proceedings, where all details are explained. Thus the main goal of the presentation is to spark the interest of the audience to read the paper, rather than dig into technical details. In general, the presenter's goal is to raise the audience interest in the work and convey the idea that the work is original, significant, and rigorous.

After preparing a public presentation, before delivering it in the real setting, it should be rehearsed in a controlled setting. Most likely, this leads to further iterations that aim at improving it. Like technical papers, a presentation is seldom right on the first try. It may improve through a careful revision process. Box 4.3 provides some additional tips on how to make effective presentations.

The previous discussion raises an important point: researchers are often exposed to feedback from others. Sometimes a draft paper or an initial presentation gets torn apart from the advisor or other colleagues. It can be excruciating, but it is also a path to improvement. One should be humble, and accept criticism. Standing in front of others is always an act of strength, not weakness.

Another skill that may be key for many kinds of research is *building artifacts*. Unless one does purely theoretical research, in all other kinds of research there is a constructive component that requires building artifacts. An artifact may be needed to implement and run experiments, to support proofs of concept, or to support validation by case studies. The ability to combine conceptual with more practical work, bridging theory to implementation, is increasingly valued in research. We discussed in Sect. 3.6 that artifacts are becoming a first-class means of diffusion. We also observed that, by sharing artifacts, researchers can make research progress faster. Since artifacts are mainly shared as software (data sets and programs), the principles of good software design and implementation need to be mastered by a PhD candidate.

A final important skill is *networking*; that is, the ability to connect and cooperate within the research community. Paraphrasing the famous poem Devotions upon Emergent Occasions by John Donne[2], "no researcher is an island entire of itself." PhD candidates must realize that connecting to the network of researchers who work on similar topics is essential for their current work and for their future. They should know who are the active researchers working in their specific area and what they are currently working on. This may allow them to know about an on-going research even before its results become published. Participating in workshops or conferences is perhaps the best way to establish connections. The advisor may help a PhD candidate to get in touch with peers doing related work, and this may allow him to get feedback on what he is doing. The external experts one connects with may be invited later to become members of the student's thesis committee (if the department has this tradition). The ability to establish connections in the research community may eventually be very useful after the PhD student finishes. Through these connections, one may find opportunities for post-doc positions. One may also get in touch with, and become known to, senior researchers who can write support letters for future appointment or promotion applications.

4.4   The Independent Researcher

In this section I try to answer the following question: what happens after completing a PhD program? A PhD degree can be the doorway into research, but one can also choose to capitalize on the gained experience in other directions, like teaching, or consulting. Others may choose to start a personal entrepreneurial adventure, or move to industry to lead development of new products, or bring innovation into practice.

---

[2]John Donne's incipit of Meditation XVII says "No man is an island entire of itself".

Box 4.3: Technical Presentation Tips

This box provides some practical tips on how to prepare the slides used in a technical presentation:

- Plan your presentation based on the time you have. Because the presentation uses slides, the allocated time constrains the number of slides you can reasonably present. Although this very much depends on the presenter's style, as a rule-of-thumb, I suggest an average of no more than two and no less than one per minute. In addition, don't overload slides with too much information. Otherwise the audience is disoriented by the continuous slide changes and cannot anchor the flow of discourse to visual information.
- Don't overdo with fancy features. Although you are trying to "sell" your research, a presentation is not a sale pitch where you have to astound the audience. You are communicating science. As a corollary, use animation wisely. Animation can be very useful, but it should not be abused.
- Be stylistically consistent. Don't change fonts, font sizes, or font colors randomly. Don't use inconsistent ways of animating slides, such as text fragments that blur, fly-in, fade,...
- Make slides readable. Be careful on the choice of colors, and make sure they are clearly visible. Make sure that the font size makes texts readable to all people in the audience.
- Don't clutter your slides with long texts. Reading long texts while the speaker is presenting can be very distracting.
- Number your slides. Someone in audience might ask a questions regarding a specific point in your presentation, and referring to the slide number can be very helpful.
- Use builds when necessary. A build looks like a slide that progressively partly changes as the presenter speaks: parts appear, parts disappear, ...
- Prepare to handle questions. Some questions may be anticipated, and extra (hidden) slides can be prepared to answer them. Rehearsal of a presentation is also important to prepare for questions. When you answer, stay cool and be concise.

If one decides to continue to do research, one can do that in industry, in public or private research centers, or in academia. Hereafter I mainly discuss what happens in this last case, although part of what I say may also apply to the other cases. It is also possible for a researcher to start her career in academia, and then move to industry. Or vice-versa, but perhaps less common, move from industry to academia. One can also decide to abandon research, and move to a different kind of business. Nothing is carved in stone.

A fresh PhD looking for an academic job as a researcher is likely to be offered first a temporary *post-doc* position. This is indeed becoming increasingly common, although it is also possible to move directly into an academic position. A post-doc position may be a good opportunity to enrich one's experience in a different context and strengthen the CV (an abbreviation from Latin *Curriculum Vitae*). Often a post-doc position gives an opportunity to the fresh PhD to supervise students, do independent teaching, and also some independent research. These are further skills one needs to develop, which may lack in PhD programs. The post-doc position may also help extending the personal collaboration network.

At some later stage, a young researcher looks for a career path in academia leading to a more stable and independent position. Different academic systems around the world have a different organization and provide different opportunities. It is thus hard to give a univocal, coherent presentation of how this transition can happen. Understanding how different hiring systems work is a necessary prerequisite for a young researcher to move along this path. In most cases, academic positions are offered by departments through open calls, and candidates must apply and compete with other applicants. Selection of candidates is often done by ad-hoc committees, whose composition may also vary from system to system, and even case to case. Committees may be composed of only local members of the department, only external members, or a mix. Success of the application depends on the applicant's qualification emerging from the material supplied with the application.

The application material is normally structured as specified by the application's requirements, which are public. Usually, it consists of a set of one or more documents, which illustrate the *portfolio* of the applicant's accomplishments. Box 4.4 discusses the main elements a research portfolio should highlight.

When first hired in academia as a junior faculty member, in most cases one is on a temporary position, and is only moved to a permanent position after a probation period and an explicit evaluation. The permanent position is often called *tenure*. Tenure is meant to protect scientists from being fired without cause, guaranteeing them academic freedom, which includes the right to research and teach any topic. The *tenure track* is a path to promotion through which a junior faculty can be moved to a permanent position and then promoted to the various levels of the academic career available at a given institution. The tenure track exists in most North American universities, and also in other countries around the world. However, other kinds of academic systems exist in different countries. A difference also exists in the kinds and numbers of levels through which an academic can progress in her career, and the mechanisms used for promotion. For example, three professorship levels are quite common in many parts of the world. In North America, they are called Assistant Professor, Associate Professor, and Full Professor; other names are used elsewhere. Different levels correspond to different responsibilities, duties, stand, and salary. It is impossible to describe here all the different regimes, or even enumerate them. In most cases, however, promotions are not automatic, but based on an explicit evaluation of merit.

Before discussing promotion, let me focus on the additional skills one should acquire and demonstrate to become a tenured scientist and progress successfully

Box 4.4: Application Material for a Junior Academic Position

The main element of an applicant's portfolio is the *publication record*, from which the quality and promise of the candidate's research should clearly emerge. The publication record should not simply be provided as a flat list of published papers, but should be enriched by elements that help interpret the list. The candidate should indicate which are the most important papers and what are their main contributions. She should highlight papers that received special recognition (e.g., the "best paper" nomination or award from a conference) or have had demonstrable impact (e.g., it is well cited, it inspired further work by other researchers, or it received a good public review, or it contributed to the development of a product). If a research was developed and published in collaboration with other researchers from other institutions, the candidate should put in evidence her collaboration network. Artifacts developed should be cited, with evidence on their (potential) use. The same holds for possible patents. If a researcher has a funding track, it should be put into proper evidence.

Another useful element of the portfolio is the applicant's *research statement*, in which the candidate describes the plan she has in mind for future independent research. The research statement should convince that the applicant has a vision that may guide her future progress as an independent researcher. The applicant might discuss how her plan fits within the department, and which new opportunities she sees knowing the department's competences. She might also discuss her plan to acquire funding to support her research.

Because teaching is an essential component of academic life, the applicant should provide some evidence of her teaching skills, in terms of past experience (which is often admittedly quite limited for a junior applicant) and a teaching plan for the future, often in a separate document called *teaching statement*.

Finally, the candidate should provide some evidence of personal service contributions, such as reviewing for journals or conferences, organizational role in scientific meetings, or participation in academic committees. Service experience is understandably limited for junior applicants.

through promotions. First, and most important, is *independence*, that is personal responsibility in defining goals and plans. Independence in research implies the ability to decide autonomously which research directions should be explored and how. This, in turn, almost inevitably implies that one should have ways to acquire the necessary financial resources to support research. Resources may be needed for the acquisition of experimental equipment, computing facilities, new devices, and so on. They are needed to support travel to participate in conferences or visit other research sites. They may be needed to support the researcher's salary (in some cases, the salary does not cover 100% of the researcher's time). Last, and most important, they may be needed to support scholarships to offer to potential PhD students to work with. Resources are rarely automatically available to the researcher. Rather they are mainly acquired through participation in *competitive funding programs*, often supported by public money, but also by other sources (e.g., industry or private foundations). The ability to compete successfully in funding acquisition is key for researchers. Demonstrable success in attracting funding is one of the important achievements taken into account when a researcher is evaluated.

It is impossible to discuss exactly what one should do to compete successfully in a competitive funding program. A possible advice heavily depends on different programs, and different programs may differ in many possible dimensions. For example, some programs support individual researchers, while others support collaborative research involving several principal investigators. Some programs focus on long-term research, while others require the applicant to collaborate with industry, and also to envision an exploitation plan for the research. Sometimes the funding program gives complete freedom to the applicant to choose the topic. In other cases, the possible topics are—more or less strictly—predefined. Before even considering applying for funding, a researcher should clearly understand the rules of the game. If one decides to do so, one should learn how to write an application that matches the purpose of the funding. It may be quite useful to look at previous successful applications, if they are publicly available, or talk to previous successful applicants.

Another important skill one should acquire and demonstrate is *advising* (or *supervising*) students. Very often, as mentioned earlier, the availability of research funds is a pre-condition for hiring students, typically PhD students. Advising students is extremely important for a researcher. It is the primary process that produces the future generation of researchers and it is a way to amplify the advisor's research breadth and depth. Sometimes researchers are initiated to advising when they are PhD students and they co-supervise Bachelor or Master students. They may be asked by their mentor to co-supervise PhD students when they work as post-docs. Co-supervision with an experienced senior faculty may be an excellent way to start, and to learn, the art of advising students. At some stage, however, a young faculty needs to take direct responsibility of an advisory role.

The art of advising students, in particular PhD students, is mainly learned by experience and by observing and capitalizing on the best practices followed by successful supervisors. Reflecting on own previous experience also helps: when one starts as a junior faculty, one should critically assess what worked well and what did not work as well when he was a PhD student. In addition, one should look for role models among other faculties in the department, and consider what can be learned from them. Learning (and improving) then continues along the entire researcher's career. As I mentioned in Box 4.2, being an accomplished scientist does not imply being a good advisor.

A prerequisite of a successful supervision is scientific strength both of the supervisor and of the student. However, a strong senior researcher pairing with a technically strong and creative student does not guarantee success. As discussed earlier, other factors, of social and psychological nature, are equally important to establish and sustain a successful relation. Successful supervisors establish a long-term relation with their students, which continues after the students progress in their career. The relation goes in both directions: students learn from the advisor, but also advisors learn from students. David A. Patterson, who has been for many years a Professor at UC Berkeley and was a recipient of the prestigious Turing Award in 2017, summarizes his experience with these beautiful words: "your students are your legacy" [41]. In the same paper, Patterson provides some thoughtful tips on advising, which are briefly summarized in Box 4.5.

Teaching is a fundamental skill that should also improve over time. Teaching is a key aspect of academic life. This book only touches teaching tangentially, as part of a researcher's life progress. Thus I only provide a few comments. Teaching requires continuous dedication and time. Teaching material needs to undergo continuous revisions and changes, especially in rapidly evolving fields. Teaching methods also change. The trend towards more active learning and use of technology (for example, on-line teaching material) are moving teaching from the traditional "ex-cathedra" style to a hands-on, participative style. Young academics need to take the lead of these changes and contribute to provide more effective teaching approaches. They should treat teaching as an opportunity—to learn more, to innovate it, to attract students—rather than a chore.

Service is another important skill that needs to develop over time. Researchers are expected to invest part of their time and effort into service activities. Junior researchers must learn how engage in service activities and at the same time they need to allocate their efforts into teaching and research. Time management becomes crucial to do these tasks well and keep stress under control. Services can be internal, in the department or college, or external. Internal service may concern participating in committees (for example, for student admission) or, in the case of more senior faculties, even take leadership roles (for example, director of undergraduate studies, or department chair). External roles may concern reviewing papers for conferences or journals, participating in editorial boards or conference committees, participating in reviewing or in selection committees of research funding programs, and so on. Remember that research organization is largely self-managed by researchers, who are expected to devote part of their time and effort to sustain community activities. The level and kind of involvement in service activities varies quite a lot according to seniority. Senior researchers are expected to spend more of their time and take more responsibilities than young researchers. Certain activities, like reviewing, are typically shared by young researchers and may be career launchers for more visible roles and additional responsibilities.

A last skill I wish to comment on is *networking*. I already mentioned networking as one of the skills a PhD student should start to develop. Networking should be further strengthened as a researcher progresses in career. Networking allows a researcher to participate in collaborative research that involves multiple participant sites. Multi-site collaborative research is increasingly common today in many funding programs. It enables the researcher's group, in particular PhD students, to be exposed to external collaborations and scientific exchanges with other groups.

Box 4.5: Tips on Student Advising

David A. Patterson provides excellent advices to advisors in [41]. I summarize his main points in my own words:

1. Provide an environment where students can develop "research taste", where they can get feedback from others, where several exciting projects are on-going. The environment should foster "camaraderie and enthusiasm." Research retreats (e.g., twice a year, for 2 or 3 days) are an excellent way of fostering this spirit. An *open collaborative laboratory* can be a physical implementation of the envisioned environment.
2. In the one-to-one interaction with a student:

   - Bolster self-confidence, which may be a problem especially for beginning students and underrepresented groups.
   - Practice public presentations by all (students and faculties). This is a good practice which both improves the student's capability and favors interaction in the research group.
   - Spend time with your students on a regular basis, for example once a week. The fixed schedule helps the students prepare for the meeting, focusing on what they need to report and on the feedback they would like to get.
   - In particular circumstances, for example during the preparation of a paper to be submitted to a conference, define with your students a schedule that allows you to provide the necessary feedback.
   - Be a trusted counselor for students when they ask for personal advice.
   - Help them if they are not making (enough) progress. Sometimes a capable student does not go deep enough in his work and comes to think that "good enough" is ok. Sometimes a student gets stuck after an initial progress. Sometimes, a student is not making any significant progress. In all these cases, an advisor must talk to the student in a frank conversation and help him decide what is best and how to proceed. It may happen that the best choice is to quit and make a different professional choice that is a better match with the individual's capabilities and skills.

For additional first-hand advices on being a successful adviser, I also recommend reading [62].

Let us now go back to *promotion*, the mechanism through which researchers progress in their career. The skills I just mentioned should be demonstrated in any promotion case, as appropriate for the specific level. To be promoted, researchers are evaluated. I discuss evaluation in depth in Chap. 5. For our present discussion, I focus here on how one should prepare for promotion evaluation. First, a candidate for promotion should understand exactly what he is evaluated for and what he is expected to have achieved. To anticipate the assembly of a *promotion dossier*, it is advisable to keep a detailed, updated record of accomplishments, to avoid collecting them in a rush, as a last minute activity. The dossier should include: CV, comprehensive research portfolio (including list of publications, grants, patents, future plans), student supervision record, comprehensive teaching portfolio, awards and recognitions, university service, external service.

4.5 Conclusions: Why Become a Researcher?

I would like to conclude this chapter with a more personal note. Why should one become researcher? What are the main motivations? What are the main expectations? Many possible answers can be given to these questions, also because there are not only many areas of research, but also many kinds of researchers. We discussed earlier many possible different personalities. The motivations and expectations vary quite substantially among them. However, I would say that there are also some commonalities. Researchers are attracted by intellectual work, problem solving, and critical thinking. They appreciate living in an international setting with no barriers, intrinsically multicultural, and open to diversity. They believe in freedom of ideas. They are passionate about their work and find it intellectually rewarding. Last but not least, becoming rich is not their top priority. They would have followed other career paths if this was top priority. They value knowledge and recognition more. The following citation from L. Da Ponte's libretto for W.A. Mozart's "Le Nozze di Figaro":

> Molto onor, poco contante (winning honours, but little money)

which was meant by the author to apply to the page Cherubino, who is leaving to become a soldier, equally applies indeed to researchers in modern times.

4.6 Further Reading

P.B. Medawar—a famous immunologist who won the Nobel prize in Medicine in 1960—wrote a delightful book on advice to a young scientist [34], which is classic and a highly recommended reading. A similar approach, and complementary issues, are discussed in [58]. Several books have also been written to provide specific advices to PhD students: for example, [13, 18].

Chapter 5
Research Evaluation

This chapter focuses on research evaluation. Evaluation is an essential aspect of research. It is ubiquitous and continuous over time for researchers. Its main goal is to ensure rigor and quality through objective assessment at all levels. It is the fundamental mechanism that regulates the highly critical and competitive research processes. To achieve its goals, it should foster fairness and minimize bias and arbitrariness.

Research findings are subject to an in-depth, critical evaluation by researchers themselves as part of their research, before they may claim that results represent acceptable theories or valid research results. Research outputs are evaluated for readiness for dissemination by peer review. Further evaluation of research results occurs over time by other researchers and by users of those results. Test of time may recognize contributions that had real impact on other research or on practice.

Evaluation may also refer to future research, when a proposal is submitted for funding, to ensure that money is spent in the best possible way. An individual's research is evaluated when one applies for an open position in a department or for promotion. Academic departments activate evaluation procedures to ensure that their limited resources are invested in productive researchers and to keep the level of their scientific reputation high. Research performance of a research institution may also be evaluated, for example to inform decisions that lead to resource allocations. Universities may do that for their departments, and even governments may do that for research institutions that receive public funding, to ensure their accountability.

The result of evaluation can be the return of a verdict—for example, in the case of promotion to a tenured position or when an application is submitted to a research funding program. Its goal, however, is more general: to sustain research quality. Evaluations should always be constructive: they should identify the strengths to promote, the possible weaknesses to compensate, and the possible areas of improvement.

Evaluation is done by experts through informed judgement. Judgement is largely based on *qualitative evaluation*. For example, in our discussion on evaluation of research papers, I argued for three main qualitative criteria: originality, significance,

© Springer Nature Switzerland AG 2020
C. Ghezzi, *Being a Researcher*, https://doi.org/10.1007/978-3-030-45157-8_5

and rigor. Because they are qualitative criteria, they are intrinsically subjective, open to unconscious bias, and the outcome of their assessment may vary across different experts who perform the evaluation and different subjects being evaluated. To mitigate subjectivity problems, normally evaluation is performed by a group of reviewers and suitable mechanisms are put in place to try to reconcile possible differences. In some cases, explicit consensus processes are put in place to expose the possibly different viewpoints to all evaluators, who then try to reach a shared assessment. There are even cases where reviewers go through an initial trial application of the review and the consensus procedure to calibrate their individual assessment criteria. We have seen an example of a simple evaluation process involving multiple reviewers in the case of journal submissions. In this case, the synthesis of the various evaluations is largely in the hands of the editors, who interpret the reviewers' reports and synthesize a decision. In the case of conferences, consensus is reached through discussions that may involve the entire program committee.

In an attempt to reduce subjectivity, which is intrinsic in qualitative evaluation, some people tried to develop *quantitative evaluation* criteria. Quantitative criteria are apparently appealing. By adopting quantitative criteria, one would expect to achieve objective evaluations, which potentially eliminate bias and arbitrariness. If the result of a quantitative analysis may be reliably expressed by a number, it can provide an indisputable way of comparing one subject against another. Furthermore, it can produce a *ranking* when it is applied to a set of subjects.

This chapter is organized as follows. Section 5.1 discusses the main principles of evaluation that should guide peer review of research outputs, focusing on scientific papers. Section 5.2 discusses the evaluation of researchers, while Sect. 5.3 focuses on evaluation of research proposals. In these sections, I mainly illustrate the viewpoint of the evaluator, complementing the discussions presented in Chap. 4, which takes the viewpoint of the subject being evaluated. I introduce quantitative evaluation criteria in Sect. 5.4 and I discuss how they should be used. I show their severe limitations, which—despite their current and increasing popularity—raise more problems than they can actually solve. I advise against their blind adoption as objective metrics. I argue that they will never be able to replace qualitative human judgement: they may instead be used with caution as data points, subject to expert interpretation.

5.1 Evaluation of Research Papers

Researchers, and even late-stage PhD students, are often asked to review technical papers submitted for publication to a journal or a conference. In Sect. 3.4, I mentioned that reviewing papers is one of the important services every scientist is supposed to deliver to the research community. When invited to review a paper, a researcher should accept to do it, unless she is not competent to review the paper, or she is objectively overloaded by other commitments that would not allow her to do a good job. If the request is accepted, she should allocate enough time to perform the review.

In the case of a conference, a researcher should accept to become a member of the program committee only if she can ensure that the papers assigned can be properly reviewed within the defined time frame. Being on a program committee is serious commitment, not just an honor. In the case of journal, when a researcher accepts the request to review a paper, she commits upfront to completing the assigned task within a deadline. The deadline can be often negotiated with the journal's editor who extended the invitation to review. Although the deadline is not as strict as for conferences, this is also a strong commitment, since delays in the publication process hamper progress of research and can damage the authors' career.

Reviewing papers, like writing papers, is hard. It requires skills that develop through experience and exposure to best practices. PhD advisors and mentors should feel responsible for helping junior researchers in the development of their reviewing skills. Not all papers are of the same kind, and the reviewer should assess the paper against criteria that pertain to the paper at hand. Box 5.1 provides an example of a characterization of the different categories into which papers can fall and the specific evaluation criteria that are appropriate for them.[1]

Reviewers' reports should deliver an informative assessment, which is directed to two kinds of recipients: the authors and either the editor in charge of the paper, in the case of a journal submission, or the conference committee, in the case of a conference paper. The editor or the conference committee in the end must decide whether the paper deserves being published. For journal papers, the decision may also be a request to the authors for a (major or minor) revision, followed by a further review step before deciding. Editors and conference committees, however, ask reviewers to tell them more than just a recommendation regarding acceptance, rejection, or revision. They need to know why a reviewer has reached that decision.

The authors, however, are the ultimate recipients. Understandably, their immediate reaction looks at the final decision about publication of their work. But they do not expect only a verdict: they also expect the review to provide a constructive feedback. The authors invested a significant amount of time and effort in the production of the paper. When they submit an article, they believe it is ready for publication. This is why the reviews are read very carefully by authors. Both in the case where the evaluation is positive and in the case where criticisms are raised, they expect comments that justify the final recommendation and also specific and constructive advice on improving their paper. In producing their reports, reviewers should always remember that they have power over the authors: their decisions can ultimately affect the authors' career progress, not to mention their self-esteem.

Most journals and conferences provide templates to guide reviewers in their evaluations. It is often possible for reviewers to provide any additional material they feel beneficial for the authors. For example, in the case of a journal submission,

---

[1] Notice that the taxonomy presented in Box 5.1 does not cover all kinds of scientific papers. As an example, it does not cover survey papers, which normally are not submitted to a conference.

Box 5.1: Review Criteria for Different Kinds of Papers

The International Conference on Software Engineering (ICSE) in 2014 adopted the following classification of submissions and described specific review criteria for the different classes. The classification is reported here as a possible guidance. It is not exhaustive and should not be viewed as a checklist. Although it refers to software engineering, it can be generalized and adapted to other research areas:

Analytical papers: A paper in which the main contribution relies on new algorithms or mathematical theory. Examples include new bug prediction techniques, model transformations, algorithms for dynamic and static analysis, and reliability analysis. Such a contribution must be evaluated with a convincing analysis of the algorithmic details, whether through a proof, complexity analysis, or run-time analysis, among others and depending on the objectives.

Empirical papers: A paper in which the main contribution is the empirical study of a software engineering technology or phenomenon. This includes controlled experiments, case studies, and surveys of professionals reporting qualitative or quantitative data and analysis results. Such a contribution will be judged on its study design, appropriateness and correctness of its analysis, and threats to validity. Replications are welcome.

Technological papers: A paper in which the main contribution is of a technical nature. This includes novel tools, modeling languages, infrastructures, and other technologies. Such a contribution does not necessarily need to be evaluated with humans. However, clear arguments, backed up by evidence as appropriate, must show how and why the technology is beneficial, whether it is in automating or supporting some user task, refining our modeling capabilities, improving some key system property, etc.

Methodological papers: A paper in which the main contribution is a coherent system of broad principles and practices to interpret or solve a problem. This includes novel requirements elicitation methods, process models, design methods, development approaches, programming paradigms, and other methodologies. The authors should provide convincing arguments, with commensurate experiences, why a new method is needed and what the benefits of the proposed method are.

Perspective papers: A paper in which the main contribution is a novel perspective on the field as a whole, or part thereof. This includes assessments of the current state of the art and achievements, systematic literature reviews, framing of an important problem, forward-looking thought pieces, connections to other disciplines, and historical perspectives. Such a contribution must, in a highly convincing manner, clearly articulate the vision, novelty, and potential impact.

Papers may belong to more than one category. Note that papers from any research area can fall into any of these categories, as the categories are constructed surrounding methodological approaches, not research topics (e.g., one could write an analytical paper on a new analysis technique, an empirical paper that compares a broad range of such techniques, a technological paper that makes an analysis technique practically feasible and available, or a perspectives paper that reviews the state of the art and lays out a roadmap of analysis techniques for the future).

a reviewer might wish to submit an annotated copy of the paper with in-line comments. This may be very useful for authors. Review templates often ask reviewers to express evaluations using both synthetic, numeric scales and detailed textual comments. The latter are always requested: numbers should always be justified by precisely stated arguments. The templates may break down evaluation into categories, and ask reviewers to score the paper against them. The indicated categories usually correspond to, or are subsumed by, originality, significance, and rigor. In addition, the quality of the *presentation* must be evaluated. This includes two aspects: *organization* and *writing style*. Organization refers to the structure of the presentation; for example, whether the needed assumptions are given before they are used, there are no unnecessary details and no redundancies, the flow of discourse is clear. A clear structure helps to make the information in the paper available to the reader with reduced effort. Proper writing style refers instead to use of scholarly vocabulary and grammar, and a polished presentation.

All review templates ask the referee to provide a final recommendation. For conference papers, usually the recommendation can score in a range from *"strong accept"* to *"strong reject"*. For a journal paper, the review may suggest one of the following: *accept, reject, major revision*, or *minor revision*. A revision should be requested if the reviewer believes that the submitted paper can be turned into an acceptable contribution. The revision can be minor or major, depending on the amount and criticality of work the authors need to invest. The reviewer should provide a list of required improvements that would turn the paper into an acceptable one. Figure 5.1 shows an example of a review template for conference papers.

Review templates also ask reviewers to self-assess their confidence, by rating how well-versed they are in the subject area. This is important to weigh the reliability of the assessment and of the feedback provided to the authors. Editors (or conference committees) should take the referee's confidence into account to orient their final decision.

The largest section of a review reports should be an assessment of the work, where the reviewers address the authors to comment on their work and on the way it is reported. Reviewers should never forget that they speak to learned peers. They should be polite and never use inflammatory tones. There is no reason for being rude, even with poor submissions. Reviewers should also consider that authors often do not write in their native language. Although they may do their best to write in a correct style, they may still make mistakes that can be easy to fix. The other important caveat is that all criticisms should be constructive and justified. For example, if the reviewer believes that what the paper presents as a new finding is actually already known, the review statement "this has been done before" would not be adequate. One should instead say "this finding was described in an earlier paper by XXX" and should provide a reference. As another example, saying "the paper lacks validation" while, for example, the paper has a section describing validation by extensive simulations would be unacceptable. If the reviewer believes that validation by simulation is not adequate, he should clearly motivate why. Likewise, one should not simply say "the paper is badly structured", but should instead explain why

Paper and reviewer information

Title:

Authors:

PC member:

Subreviewer:	First name	_____
	Last name	_____
	Email address	_____

Evaluation

Overall evaluation. Both an overall evaluation and a detailed review are required.

◯ 3: strong accept

◯ 2: accept

◯ 1: weak accept

◯ 0: borderline paper

◯ -1: weak reject

◯ -2: reject

◯ -3: strong reject

Detailed comments: Please support your overall evaluation by commenting on originality, significance, rigor, and presentation

Reviewer's confidence

◯   5: (expert)
◯   4: (high)
◯   3: (medium)
◯   2: (low)
◯   1: (none)

Confidential remarks for the program committee.

Fig. 5.1 A review template for a conference paper

the structure is wrong and why it hampers readability, and should suggest a better structure.

There are cases in which the work to review is out scope, or it is a very badly written paper, or it has fundamental and insurmountable flaws. In these cases, the reviewer can avoid providing a detailed review report and should indicate why this is not possible. In the end, it is the responsibility of the author to meet certain minimal standards before reviewing can take place. Sometimes, editors can desk-reject a paper without sending it out for review if they are confident that the paper is fatally flawed. In the specific case of journal papers that are based on previous conference publications, the reviewers should consider the relationship between the submission and the previous conference versions, and make sure that the submission provides enough new contribution, also in accordance with the journal's policies and in consultation with the editor.

Reviews are often done and written incrementally, and they undergo revisions before they are finalized. A possible strategy is to go quickly through the whole paper once, to get an overall impression, and then do additional passes to get into the details. When it comes to writing the review report, reviewers should seriously ask themselves two questions, as a sanity check before submission. The first question is: What would my reaction be if I would receive this review? The second is: If the reviewer's name would be disclosed to the authors or appear in public, would I be embarrassed? If the answer is "yes" to one of these two questions, then the report should be rewritten.

To summarize, the review process must be taken very seriously, both by reviewers and authors. Reviewers behave honestly and apply their best judgement. Authors should never abuse the system. They should only submit work that has been carefully self-evaluated in terms of contents and presentation. When they receive reviews, they should take them very seriously. In particular, this is very crucial if they are asked to re-submit their paper after revision. This last point is very important, and it is further discussed in Box 5.2.

5.2 Evaluation of Researchers in Their Careers

A scientist's research record is evaluated in all his major career steps. Hereafter I consider two cases that are quite standard: evaluation in the case of hiring for a junior non-permanent position and evaluation for promotion to a permanent position. Scientists are also evaluated when they compete for research funding by submitting an application to a funding program. This is also an important case of evaluation that can affect the researcher's career. I briefly comment on it in Sect. 5.3.

The academic processes of hiring and promotion vary a lot across countries and institutions, although the basic structure and the objectives also have lots of similarities. I provide an overall view by referring to rather typical, but idealized processes. Before going through these processes, a researcher should clearly understand the specific details.

Box 5.2: Tips on Paper Revision and Resubmission

Let us consider a journal submission for which the authors received a request for a minor or a major revision. When submitting their revised work for further review, the authors should also provide a written report describing how the revision took the review reports into consideration. They should do that by explicitly referring to the editor's assessment and to each reviewer's report. They should write a section for each reviewer, in which they go through every point in the reviewer's report and clearly explain if they agree or disagree with the request or comment. In case they disagree, they should politely explain why. In case they agree, they should indicate how the revised text has been changed.

The tone of the report should be thankful and respectful. In cases where reviewers misunderstood the authors' point, it is very likely that the original text did not help the reader avoid misinterpretations. If a reviewer has given particularly useful comments or has spotted flaws in the original manuscript, the authors should express their gratitude. To facilitate communication with the reviewers, the authors should make it easy to trace the relevant changes between the original and the revised submission, for example using a light-grey background instead of white to indicate the changed portions of text.

In some cases, conferences may also allow some limited forms of interaction between authors and reviewers, typically by allowing authors' to submit rebuttals to the reviews, before the final decision to accept or reject submissions is made by the program committee. The rebuttal stage follows strict rules defined by the program committee. Because of hard time constraints, the rebuttal may be length-limited (typically, 500 or 1000 words) and authors may have only a few days to produce a response. This is the only chance given to the authors to respond to the reviews before the final decision. Rebuttals should be crafted very carefully and focus on the key points, since authors must comply normally with severe space constraints.

Let us focus first on research evaluation for a candidate who applies for a junior tenure-track position. The goal is to select the applicant who shows more promise for growth towards a research leadership role. The candidate's research area should fit the criteria listed in the call for applications, which reflect the department's development strategy to invest in certain areas. It can also happen that an outstanding applicant may be chosen even if her area does not quite match the call. We saw earlier that evaluation does not just focus on research, but research performance is by far more important than any other aspect, like service and teaching, for junior recruitments. The evaluation, which leads to a decision, may be made by an ad-hoc committee, by a collegial departmental decision, or by a combination of them. There are cases where evaluation and decision are two distinct processes handled by different bodies: an ad-hoc committee composed of external members provides an evaluation report to the decision body (for example, the department).

The evaluation is made on the basis of the application material provided by candidates, as discussed in Chap. 4, support letters from independent experts, oral presentations, and interviews.

A screening of applicants is often performed as a first step of the evaluation process, based on the application material. The goal is to narrow down the set of candidates to a manageable number. Publications play a key role. Reviewers are expected to read carefully the most relevant publications submitted by each applicant, to form their personal opinion of the applicant's research strengths. Reviewers should also look for support to their opinion by looking at other sources of objective evidence. For example, they may take into account the prestige and selectivity of the publication venues. They can try to get evidence of impact of the work, considering for example best paper nominations, citations, and other kinds of recognition (e.g., external uses of artifacts, patents, startup initiatives, etc.). Teaching and research statements articulate the candidate's strategy for future developments in these two areas, and how those strategies may fit into, and contribute to, the department. The statements should be assessed as indicators of the applicant's maturity: how well prepared the applicant is to undertake an independent journey as a faculty member.

Reference letters are asked by the hiring department to experts in the specific research area of the candidate. Experts are selected among reputable senior researchers, also taking into consideration a list of potential references provided by candidates. References are asked to provide a candid assessment of the candidate, to position the candidate among other scientists with the similar seniority in the same research area, and to comment about qualification and potential for further development.

Box 5.3 provides some tips on how to write reference letters. These tips should be of interest to those who may be asked to write letters. Researchers who need reference letters may also be interested, to understand what a reference letter should say and how it may affect a decision regarding their application.

5.3 Evaluation of Research Proposals

Research funding is seldom provided to researchers as a bonus. By and large, it has to be obtained by external sources, often through highly competitive processes. Funding programs are launched by public organizations, such national funding agencies, non-profit foundations, or from industry. They may differ quite substantially in the degree of openness of research objectives, orientation to specific target results, and ownership of the results by the researcher. Certain funding programs are extremely competitive and prestigious: success in the competition is considered as an important achievement when a researcher is evaluated. For example, in the USA the National Science Foundation CAREER awards and in the EU the European

Box 5.3: Tips on Writing Reference Letters

Writing reference letters is one of the skills researchers should learn. Researchers may be asked to write letters to recommend their students who apply for admission in other programs, to support hiring or promotion cases, or to support nominations of colleagues for certain roles or awards. There are obvious differences among all these cases. Here I mainly focus on reference letters for junior researchers applying for an initial position.

Writing a reference letter requires honest judgement, time, and dedication. When asked by an applicant to be named as a possible reference, it is advisable to accept only if one expects the recommendation to be demonstrably supportive. Otherwise, I would suggest to kindly decline. If nominated as a reference by an institutional body (for example, a department), one should feel a moral obligation to accept, as a service to the community.

Letters should not be generic. They should clearly focus on the case for which they are written. The evaluator must become familiar with the candidate's CV and main contributions. The evaluator must also understand exactly what the person is being recommended for. A description of the open position and of the expected skills of applicants is always provided to the evaluator.

The letter should start with background information. It should provide a brief introduction of the qualification of the recommender, highlighting the factors that can give weight to the evaluation. It should also describe the relation to the candidate: Does the recommender know the candidate personally? For how long? Under what circumstances? And how did she become acquainted? For example: the recommender heard the candidate present papers in conferences, met him in a workshop and discussed personally about his research, or she can provide evidence of his technical depth and competence as a reviewer. Previous personal relations with the candidate can add a personal touch to the letter and give useful concrete evidence.

The letter should provide a truthful and detailed description of the candidate's strengths and weaknesses, and discuss fitness to the position. One should identify all the positive aspects, not through generic statements, but through concrete facts. In the case of negative remarks, they should be expressed firmly, but politely, avoiding any possible harm.

Sometimes the reviewer is asked to position the candidate within his class of peers. For example, she might be asked to say whether he is in the top 2%, 5%, or 10%, ... The letter could be more specific, comparing the candidate with significant concrete cases. For example, to stress the candidate's research strength one could refer to recent similar competitions in reputable departments where the successful candidate had comparable qualification. One may also say "If the candidate would apply for a similar position in my department, I would struggle to make him an offer."

In conclusion, the evaluation should be specific about the strengths of the candidate, which would make him special and different from other possible candidates. A letter that simply praises him without being concrete and makes him look perfect is not credible. If the candidate has weaknesses, they should be highlighted, perhaps also indicating how they might be mitigated.

Research Council (ERC) awards are considered as major achievements. The ability of a researcher to compete successfully in research funding programs is a key, decisive factor in researchers' evaluation for hiring and promotion.

Playing the role of a reviewer of research proposals is a duty for a researcher: it is a service to the community. It is a very critical activity, which can affect both the developments of science and the career of researchers. Evaluation is mainly done by peer review, and is based on assessing both the applicant's qualification and the proposed work. This typically happens in the case of competitive public funding.[2] Evaluation of the applicant aims at appraising not only the quality level of his track record, but also qualification for the proposed research. In some cases, an applicant might submit a proposal in a new area, in which he has no previous experience. In this case, the previous track record may not indicate potential success in the new area; other sources of information may be sought in other supplied material by the applicant. In general, an applicant must provide arguments to show that he is fit for the proposed research.

Evaluation of the proposed work is based on a number of criteria, often made explicit in a review template the evaluator is expected to fill. An example of a standard checklist for the evaluation of research proposals is reported in Box 5.4. Very often, competitive research funding generates a lot of competition, and the number of applicants largely exceeds the allocation of the available budget. The result of peer evaluations normally generates a ranking of fundable research projects. The final decision of which proposals should get funded might then be taken by the funding panel.

5.4   Quantitative Research Evaluation via Bibliometrics

In recent years, there has been a growing interest towards quantitative methods for research evaluation. The main motivation for this quest has been to reduce the subjectivity, potential bias, and arbitrariness inherent in purely qualitative methods. Another motivation is to reduce or even eliminate individual responsibility in evaluations, through some kind of systematic, objective, or even automated procedure. Quick and objective scoring methods look indeed very attractive to organizations as potential aids to automate complex, time consuming, and critical decision processes. It is no surprise that a rash of proposals have been made and received a lot of attention. A new field, called *bibliometrics*, has emerged. Bibliometrics has the goal of introducing a metric system to support quantitative analysis of research by focusing—as the name suggests—on publications. Several concepts introduced by bibliometrics are already widely used (and often misused) and this has generated heated controversies. The appealing side of bibliometrics is that any metric (no matter which), when applied to measure a set of subjects, leads

---

[2]Private institutions and industry may follow different schemes.

Box 5.4: Criteria to Evaluate a Research Proposal

This is a possible checklist to evaluate a research proposal:

- How well does the proposal fit the objective of the funding program? This is especially important in the case of top-down research funding programs (see Sect. 1.5), where calls are issued on very specific research targets that express some societal or industrial priority; for example, "Internet-of-Things for home automation", or "Low-emission urban transportation systems." A request for funding research that focuses on a different topic would not be acceptable, no matter how technically good the applicant and the proposal are.
- How timely and novel is the proposal? Novelty is always a key issue, and must of course be contextualized. An idea may not be novel per se, but its application in a certain context can be novel and can bring huge advantages. Timeliness can also be quite relevant, depending on the funding program. For example, the diffusion of a certain technology in real life (e.g., sensor networks for home automation) makes analysis of security threats for sensor networks a timely research area. A new compiler technique for code optimization may instead be quite novel (and technically very deep), but may not be considered timely.
- What are the concrete outputs of the research? Does it mainly promise to deliver papers? Are any other forms of dissemination or trials also planned? How do these outputs fit the objectives of research?
- What is the expected impact and of what kind? On the market, on society, on industry, on other research in the area, on other disciplines?
- How risky is the proposal? Can the proposed research deliver its expected results? Does the proposal analyze how to handle possible failure in reaching some of its objectives?
- Are the proposed research methods sound? Is the mathematical apparatus proposed by the research adequate? Is the kind of proposed validation sufficient to guarantee quality of the results?
- Is the proposed workplan credible? Suppose that the applicant proposes to use the allocated funding to hire 2 or 3 PhD students to work on different research streams. Is the time allocated to those streams credible?
- Is the requested budget justified? If the requested budget is not justified and would lead to over-funding, can the reviewer recommend a budget reduction?

to a ranking, which may then facilitate decisions about the subjects. Hereafter, I introduce the main metrics, I critically evaluate them, and I discuss their possible uses and misuses.

The proposed metric system for research quality starts from the definition of a basic metric, which is intended to capture the notion of *quality* of a scientific paper. Quality is intended as the *impact* exerted by the paper, and this is measured by the *number of citations* received. The relation between the number of citations and impact has an intuitive appeal. Citations, however, are only a crude proxy for the impact of a research paper.

There are many reasons why the plain number of citations is not a robust metric for impact. First, it is sensitive to the *time elapsed since publication*: for example, how can one compare the number of citations of a 2-year old paper and a 20-year old one? Today's citation count may grow tomorrow. There may be an inertia in the number of citations: even a very influential paper may have a small number of citations one or two years after its publication, and the number may then grow tremendously afterwards. Second, the number of citations is a noisy indicator: it may include *self-citations* and it does not define which sources are counted as valid citing subjects. These problems might be countered, but often they are not. It is in principle possible to exclude self-referenced publications from the count, but how about the unethical game played by groups who decide to cite each other with the sole aim to increase citation counts? These examples show that the number of citations is a rather poor and easy to hack indicator.

Even assuming that the problems I just mentioned are eliminated, an even more fundamental question arises: can we trust the number of citations as a robust metric to capture the notion of impact? That would presuppose a highly rational, uniform, and systematic model of reference giving. But unfortunately this is not true. A report from the International Mathematical Union provides an excellent discussion of the many pitfalls of citation counts as a metric for impact [2]. The report observes that citation practices differ quite substantially among disciplines. Citation counts cannot be used to compare research impact of contributions in different areas. In addition, citations can have different purposes, other than showing intellectual dependency on the cited. Very often, they are just a way to carry out a scientific conversation. A reference may be included in a paper to show that the topic is also of interest to someone else, or to prove that the author knows the literature. Sometimes the cited paper explains a result, not necessarily of the cited author. Sometimes a paper is cited just an exemplar of another approach, different from the one presented in the citing paper. Sometimes a citation may even express a negative credit. In conclusion, the use and meaning of citations is very subjective, which means that simply counting them does not lead to a meaningful indicator of impact for research papers.

The problem is even more serious because existing bibliometric approaches use the number of citations to build other metrics whose intended use is to provide a quantitative evaluation of other aspects of research. For example, I mentioned that many journals and conferences exist, with different degrees of scientific reputation. I also mentioned that different research communities have their reference journal and conferences, and to a large extent, communities share a consensus about reputability of their venues. Reputation of a journal or conference derives from a social process. It captures á shared view of the scientific quality of the published contributions and of their overall impact. Can a metric capture this concept in an objective manner? The notion of *impact factor* has been introduced to answer this question.

Let us consider the case of a journal. Its impact factor is defined as the yearly average number of citations to articles published in that journal. Precisely, in any given year, the impact factor of a journal is defined by the following formula:

$$IF(y) = \frac{Citations(y-1) + Citations(y-2)}{Publications(y-1) + Publications(y-2)} \tag{5.1}$$

The formula computes the impact factor of a given journal in year y as the number of citations of articles published during the two preceding years, divided by the total number of articles published in that journal during the two preceding years. Variations of this metric also exist. For example, instead of only considering 2 years, a five-year impact factor considers a period of 5 years. The notion of impact factor can also be applied to conferences.

Does the impact factor capture the notion of reputation of a journal or conference? Although in this case the count of citations is precisely scoped within a time frame, the problem of using citations as proxies for impact is still there. In addition, it has been observed that citation counts have highly skewed distributions: few papers are highly cited, while many have a small number of citations. Skewed distributions make the use of the mean number potentially misleading.

Comparing impact factors across scientific areas is also problematic. For example, one can see in Fig. 5.2 that the average citations per article in life sciences is

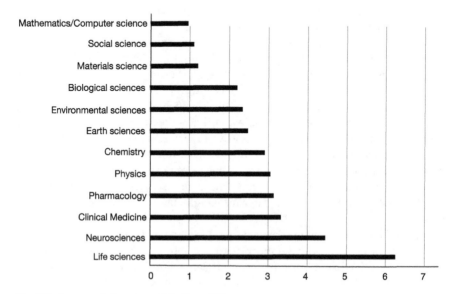

Fig. 5.2 Average citations per article (from [2])

much higher than in mathematics or informatics. The metric is also easy to tweak by
unethical editorial policies that encourage authors of accepted papers to add more
citations to papers in the same journal or conference. Finally, the metric is also
open to a subtle potential misuse: unscrupulous reviewers who are asked to assess a
researcher's publication may be tempted to rank the paper according to the impact
factor of the venue in which it appears, instead of assessing its intrinsic quality. This
is unfair. It may happen that two papers PA and PB appear in two venues A and B,
where A has higher impact factor than B. Paper PA has never been cited by others
and has very low significance, while paper PB has been recognized by the research
community as a seminal contribution.

A metric, called *H-index*, has also been introduced to evaluate researchers. The
goal of the metric is to measure, with a single number, both the productivity
and citation impact of a researcher. The metric was suggested in 2005 by Jorge
E. Hirsch, a physicist at UCSD, as a tool for determining theoretical physicists'
relative quality. It is called Hirsch index (abbreviated as H-index). It is defined as
the maximum value of h such that the given author has published h papers that
have each been cited at least h times. If we plot papers by decreasing number of
citations, computation of the H-index h is shown in Fig. 5.3. Most of the criticisms
raised earlier to other metrics apply to H-index as well, because of the controversial
underlying assumption that citation counts are a good proxy for impact of a scientific
paper. The metric blatantly favors quantity over quality. Many papers with a decent
number of citations rank a researcher higher than a few very influential, seminal,
highly cited papers. In addition, seniority plays a fundamental role in rankings based
on H-index.

Quantitative evaluation has been applied in other and broader contexts, to
evaluate and rank research and higher education institutions, at all levels: specific

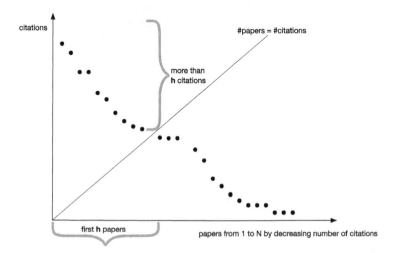

Fig. 5.3 H-index

programs, departments, schools, or even entire colleges and universities. In these cases, evaluation goes beyond just research excellence, assessed by bibliometrics. It considers also a variety of other factors, ranging from funding and endowment, specialization expertise, admissions, student options, award numbers, internationalization, graduate employment, industrial linkage, historical reputation, and other criteria. Evaluation is performed by specialized magazines and newspapers, websites, governments, or academics, instead of peer review. Although the foundations for these evaluation are questionable, they receive a lot of attention in the news, and may orient students, families, the general public, and even government decisions regarding public education. There are heated debates about usefulness and accuracy of these rankings, as well as a lack of consensus on which factors should be considered to produce reliable rankings. Despite the deficiencies and serious concerns all experts individually acknowledge, these rankings are often referenced and used unquestioningly as objective truths.

5.5 Conclusions and Recommendations: How to Survive Through Evaluations

Research undergoes evaluation processes at all times, in all its phases. Researchers are also continuously evaluated as they progress throughout their career. Evaluation is key to improving research quality and productivity. To achieve the intended beneficial effects, however, it should be performed for a well defined purpose, it should follow established principles, it should be benchmarked against appropriate criteria, and sensitive to disciplinary differences. The effect of applying wrong criteria or practices in research evaluation can have seriously negative long-term effects and damage the potential of future generations of researchers. I pointed out that in an attempt to reduce the negative effects of subjectivity, in recent years there has been an increasing reliance on bibliometrics, which tries to make evaluation objective through quantitative measures. The use of metrics has also been suggested as a possible remedy for the lack of scalability of peer review to the dramatic increase in number of researchers, number of papers, number of venues. I countered this laudable goal by presenting a critical view of the existing metrics and their use as objective quality indicators in research evaluation. Their deficiencies show that relying on them as the sole evaluation criterion would be a total disaster. They can only be used as an aid, subject to critical assessment.

To conclude this chapter, let me provide some final recommendations, inspired by a public report issued by *Informatics Europe*, the European association of academic departments and research institutions [11]. Apart from some Informatics-specific considerations, these recommendations are in line with the positions expressed by most international scientific associations in the same and also in different fields (see, for example, [16, 21, 49]).

- To achieve its positive objectives, the specific goals of any kind of evaluation must be clearly formulated upfront, and the way it is conducted must be aligned with these goals. Evaluation should follow established principles, known and shared by evaluators and researchers, and take into account any specificities of the scientific field and area involved.
- Evaluation criteria should take into account that the research diffusion culture is changing, and also differs across fields. Research is disseminated not only through journal publications, but also conferences. Digital technologies allow both artifact sharing and new forms of open dissemination. Evaluation cannot be restricted to only one kind.
- Because of the different cultures in research dissemination, the results of evaluation in one field should never be used for direct comparison with another field. For example, the publication record of a junior researcher in, say, Condensed-Matter Physics, cannot be directly compared with a junior researcher in Computer Vision. One can, instead, say that one is an emerging international star in her field and was awarded prestigious recognitions, while the other only has a good national reputation in his own field. Their research stands can only be compared indirectly through their stands in their respective fields.
- Publication counts should never be used as indicators of quality of researchers (see also [39]). They measure a form of productivity, but neither impact nor research quality.
- While evaluating researchers, factors other than citations must also be taken into account. Community recognitions are important indicators. Major conferences often grant *best paper awards* to the papers perceived to have the highest value of those accepted at a conference. Scholarly societies often grant *test-of-time awards* for the papers perceived to have had the highest influence in the area in the last—say, 10—years. They also grant awards to individual researchers for their contributions, such as *Outstanding PhD thesis*, or *Early Career Research Award*, or *Outstanding Research Award*. These distinguishing, peer reviewed awards should be highly valued in evaluation.
- Outreach efforts are another key indicator. The spectrum of possible outreach activities is wide. It can go from start-up initiatives to exploitation (or adoption) of research results by industry or standards bodies, to engagement with society in defining policies, or dissemination to the general public of research results. Outreach activities are not a substitute for research excellence, but if they can be traced back to excellent research they are a sign of impact.
- Numerical bibliometric data, such as citation counts, may provide insights and may be used to inform evaluation, but should never be used as the sole source of evaluation. Any use of these techniques must be subjected to the filter of human interpretation. Although a high number of citations to a paper, e.g., hundreds, suggests impact, this must be confirmed by direct scrutiny to assess its intellectual depth, as well as originality, significance, and rigor of the contribution. Personal judgement is needed to discriminate, for example, the case where the high number of citations is due to the survey nature of the paper or instead to the novelty and significance of the contribution. Bibliometrics can only

be a complement to personal in-depth scrutiny of all kinds of research outputs produced by a scientist.

- All bibliometric data available today must be taken with extreme care and used wisely. The value they provide for the same metric (for example, the H-index) varies across available sources. Let us consider the three main sources of bibliometric data: GoogleScholar, ISI Web of Science, and Scopus. The data sources they use to compute the various metrics differ and they may not support benchmarking. For example, they differ in the way they consider journal and conference papers, they differ in the possibility of fixing a date to compare, for example, the H-indexes of two researchers.

As a general principle, research assessment should be used to assess quality and impact over quantity. This is especially crucial when it comes to evaluating researchers for hiring and in promotion cases. Any policy that tends to favor quantity over quality has potentially disruptive effects on the development of science and may mislead young researchers, with very negative long-term effects. Such policies can lead to just focusing on easily publishable work and minimal increments over previously published material. To favor quality, researcher evaluations should rather focus on a smaller number of outputs, trying to exert impact through their novelty, significance, and supporting artifacts.

As a final comment, I would like to raise the attention on the need to shield peer evaluations from ethical misconducts. Since peer review is a human activity, it is open to misconducts that may produce serious damage. I discuss the ethical aspects of research in Chap. 6.

5.6   Further Reading

The Leiden Manifesto [21] discusses the principles that should guide research evaluation. The European University Association presents interesting reflections on university research assessment in [49]. The report [11] focuses on research evaluation in informatics. Excellent discussions of best practices for evaluating informatics researchers for promotion and tenure can be found in [16, 40]. A scholarly dissection of the use of citations as proxies for impact is presented by Adler et al. [2]. Forceful arguments against using purely quantitative assessments in research evaluation are presented by David Parnas in [39].

Chapter 6
Research Ethics

Ethics is a branch of philosophy that studies human behavior and provides rules and guidelines for individuals and for groups distinguishing between wrong and right conduct, according to an ideal behavioral model. In this chapter I discuss ethics in the context of scientific research. Researchers, as any human beings who are citizens of the world, should behave ethically: they should adhere to the common ethical principles that apply in everyday life. These include honesty, fairness, objectivity, openness, trustworthiness, respect for others, confidentiality. Reification of these principles in the research context leads to openness in sharing research results, fairness in peer review, respect for colleagues and students, honesty in reporting research results.

Ethical principles may also be operationalized by governments into *law*, to sanction certain unethical human actions which may undermine social order or endanger safe and peaceful living conditions. Ethics and law, however, differ quite substantially. Here I only focus on the individual and professional ethical principles that apply to research.

Ethical principles lead to *professional standards*, also called *codes of conduct*, which are specific for each profession. A medical code of conduct applies to physicians. This includes the Hippocratic Oath, which is the first example in history of a professional code of conduct, traced back to the Greek physician Hippocrates, who lived between the fifth and fourth centuries BC. Other examples are the code of conduct for journalists, or the code of conduct for accountants. Codes of conduct may be more or less formally defined, but they exist for most professions and they are shared by their professionals. A set of professional standards also exists for research, to which responsible researchers must adhere. *Research integrity* is adherence to the ethical principles in research. Violation is instead called *research misconduct*. More precisely, a misconduct can be defined as a departure from accepted practices committed intentionally, or knowingly, or recklessly, proven by preponderance of evidence. Violations can be more or less severe. In any case, they should never be confused with differences of opinions, dissents, or controversial positions.

© Springer Nature Switzerland AG 2020
C. Ghezzi, *Being a Researcher*, https://doi.org/10.1007/978-3-030-45157-8_6

Violations of research integrity are taken very seriously by the research community. A researcher's misconduct not only has negative consequences on the individual, but can also shed a negative light on the environment in which the researcher operates, such as the research group or the hosting institution. It may even shed a negative light on the research community.

I distinguish between ethical principles that apply to research in general, irrespective of the specific investigation area (hereafter called *topic-independent*), and those that arise specifically due to the subject area and investigation method being followed (hereafter called *topic-specific*). Topic-independent ethical principles mainly refer to the researcher's conduct in relation with students, peers, own organization, funding body, etc. This is the subject of Sect. 6.1, which discusses the principles for the individual researcher's behavior, and Sect. 6.2, which focuses on ethics in relation with other researchers. Section 6.3 instead discusses how ethical issues arise in the daily practice of research. As for topic-specific ethical principles, consider the obvious case of experimentation with humans or animals in life sciences, or observational studies of human behaviors in social sciences. Topic-specific issues are discussed in Sect. 6.4. Section 6.5 goes deeper into the ethical concerns induced by progress in Informatics. An unprecedented cyber-world is being created by advances in research and technological developments in Informatics, where humans operate and interact with and through new kinds of autonomous digital entities. New ethical questions arise. The notions of good and bad conduct, of rights and duties must be revisited and adapted to this new and rapidly evolving world.

6.1   General Ethical Principles for the Individual Researcher

A *misconduct* has been broadly defined as a violation of the ethical principles and values. How can a *research misconduct* be more precisely defined? Definitions have been provided, for example, in the The European Code of Conduct for Research Integrity [3] and by the Office of Research Integrity of the U.S. Department of Health and Human Services.[1] A research misconduct is defined as *fabrication, falsification*, or *plagiarism* (the so-called FFP categorization) in *proposing, performing*, or *reviewing* research, or in *reporting* research results. Precisely:

- *Fabrication* is making up results and recording them as if they were real.
- *Falsification* is manipulating research materials, equipment or processes, or changing, omitting, or suppressing data or results without justification, such that the research is not accurately represented in the research record.

---

[1] https://ori.hhs.gov/definition-misconduct.

- *Plagiarism* is using other people's work and ideas without giving proper credit to the original source, thus violating the rights of the original author(s) to their intellectual outputs.

Let us look closer to fabrication, falsification, and plagiarism in performing research and reporting research results. Possible misconducts can have different degrees of severity, which can range from totally unacceptable to deplorable to better to abstain from. In some cases, misconducts can be even sanctioned as law infringements, as for example in the case of plagiarism that leads to violation of an existing copyright protection law.

Fabrication is always a very serious misconduct. Making up data or results and recording or reporting them as scientific results is simply unacceptable. However, careless choice of data and reporting of poorly substantiated results may be an indication of sloppiness and lack of professionalism, which makes them lesser cases of misconduct, although they are still unacceptable. Deliberate falsification is also a serious misconduct. Consider, however, the case in which a researcher omits to report data from experiments that may shed a less favorable light on a research artifact he or she invented. This is certainly unacceptable, but it is a less severe misconduct than deliberately manipulating the data from experiments that would disprove a hypothesis. A similar case is *overselling* research results; that is, claiming that the results achieved have a much higher value that can actually be justified. Overselling is more a bad practice than a misconduct. However, it should always be avoided.

Let us now look closer to plagiarism, which—regrettably—is a rather common example of a research misconduct. Let us first focus on plagiarism of ideas. This refers to appropriation of someone's ideas in whole or in part without giving credit to the originator. An idea can be an explanation, a theory, a conjecture, a new research direction. Plagiarism of ideas may be hard to judge. In some cases, the evidence of a serious misconduct is clear. For example, a researcher (Mark) hears the presentation of a colleague (Lynda), who elaborates on a new, original idea that may lead to a new research proposal, which has potential high impact and may be favorably considered by a research funding program. The presentation is given in an informal setting, and Lynda explicitly mentions that what she presents should be treated confidentially. Then Mark uses exactly the same idea and approach as if they were his own idea and approach, without giving credit to Lynda. This is clearly unethical. The other end of the spectrum (that is, no misconduct) would be a case where very preliminary research ideas emerge informally during dinner with colleagues at a conference and one elaborates on the idea until it becomes a submittable research proposal. To describe the situation where preliminary ideas float around in informal gatherings, sometimes researchers say that these ideas are "in the air."

Researchers should never forget to give credit to peers for previous work upon which they build. For example, suppose you are solving a problem that was solved earlier by another researcher, but you provide a better solution. It would be unfair to attribute all the merit to yourself and publish your solution without giving credit to the previous contribution and without validating your solution against the previous one.

Plagiarism of text is another common misconduct in research. It amounts to copying a portion of text, possibly with cosmetic changes, from another source without giving credit or enclosing the text in a proper quotation.

A special and subtle case is *self-plagiarism*. This can range from including pieces of text (or figures, or any other material) from a paper into another by the same author, to duplicating the contents of previous papers in a new form, without citing and explaining why. In some cases, there may be a reason for reusing own previous text, which does not qualify as self-plagiarism. For example, in the case of re-stating the same background material, or when previous complex material is restated into a tutorial form, or in the case where a previous conference papers is extended and published in a journal. This sometimes happens for the best papers from a conference, when the authors are explicitly invited to submit an extended version of their work for publication in a journal. The rationale is that the journal version should include additional material that could not be included in the conference paper, due to space limitations. In all these cases, however, the authors should explain why this is done and give credit to the original contribution.

There are also cases that do not clearly qualify as self-plagiarism, but they are bad practices and should anyway be avoided. Sometimes the pressure to publish leads to the *Least Publishable Unit syndrome*, whereby researchers submit papers whose contribution with respect to previously published material is negligible or minimal, while restatement of previous work takes most of the space in the new submission.

6.2   Ethical Principles in Research Relations

Researchers do not live in a vacuum: they have relations with other researchers and operate within institutions. Additional ethical principles arise due to these relations. I discuss three main issues that are of paramount importance: conflict of interest, confidentiality, and fairness in evaluations. Violations of these principles lead to other cases of misconduct in research.

Conflict of interests can be defined in general as a situation in which an agent (an individual or an organization) is involved in multiple conflicting interests, and serving one would work against another. Specifically, we consider the case where a professional decision has to be made or an action has to be taken regarding a *primary interest*, or *principal goal*, which may be influenced by a *secondary interest*, and the conflict between the two may compromise the integrity of the decision or action. In our context, the ultimate principal goal is supporting production and dissemination of good research, while secondary interests may be personal goals of the researcher's development or the desire to favor own institution, or collaborators, or friends. The principal goal (research integrity) is mandated to researchers by their profession.

Conflict of interests occurs when the primary interest of an agent interferes with the secondary interest of another agent who has precise duties and responsibilities towards the principal goal. Typically, the agent has to express judgement or decide on behalf of the principal goal.

A classic example is the case in which an individual is part of a jury that must select one among several participants in a competition. In the context of research, a member of the program committee has to recommend acceptance or rejection of papers submitted to the conference. The primary interest (principal goal) is to choose the papers that deserve being disseminated—they reach a certain quality threshold in terms of originality, significance, and rigor—to make the conference valuable and esteemed. But suppose that one of his close collaborators submits a paper. A conflict of interests arises because the primary goal—choosing the best contributions—interferes with the secondary goal—supporting and promoting own collaborators. Other examples may arise in hiring or promoting researchers, and in evaluating funding proposals, where one may be driven by purely personal motivations—including friendship or close relation or collaboration in projects— instead of objective criteria, to favor a specific candidate.

To summarize, a conflict of interests requires three main elements:

1. An agency relation between a delegating agent and another agent; in the example the conference (viewed as an agent) delegates program committee members to evaluate and decide.
2. The presence of a secondary interest in the delegated agent; in the example, the agent aims at supporting and promoting his or her own collaborators.
3. An interference of the secondary interest with the primary interest; in the example, in the context of paper selection for a conference.

Notice that conflict of interests is an objective situation and does not per-se imply a moral judgement. Likewise, secondary interests should not be considered as wrong. What is important is to avoid any occurrence of conflict of interests when secondary interests may compromise achievement of the primary goal.

The previous discussion naturally brings to the notion of *potential conflict of interests*. A potential conflict of interests is a situation in which the secondary interest of an agent could in the future interfere with the primary interest of another agent towards whom the former has precise duties and responsibilities. A possible countermeasure to the insurgence of actual conflicts of interest consists in making the possible interests that may conflict explicit. In the example of conferences, the authors who submit papers are normally asked to indicate the members of the program committee they have conflict with. This includes colleagues from the same institution, current or recent research collaborators, past PhD students, and so on. Likewise, the members of the program committee are asked to indicate which submitted papers are authored by researchers they have conflict with. Program committee members should not review papers authored by researchers they have a potential conflict of interests with. They should not know who are the reviewers and should not participate in any discussion regarding these papers. A further example of a subtle conflict of interests is presented in Box 6.1.

> ### Box 6.1: Technical Conflict of Interests
>
> A situation that can be called *technical conflict of interests* arises when a researcher is asked to review a paper, or a research proposal, describing a new technique or approach, which competes in some way with the reviewer's own work. This situation is often hard to judge and track, and therefore it is potentially quite dangerous. As an example, the new proposal may improve or extend a previous solution by the reviewer. In principle, the reviewer is extremely well qualified to assess the work. The reviewer, however, might be both positively and negatively biased in her judgement. She might look at the work with an exceedingly positive eye, because the new proposal acknowledges her work. But she might also be exceedingly negative, feeling deprived of further developments of her original ideas.
> A reviewer should cautious about possible technical conflict of interests. Before accepting to be a reviewer, she should honestly ask herself if a potential conflict exists and immediately notify—and explain—the case to those who asked for the review. In case of any doubt, it would be wise not act as a reviewer.

Conflicts of interests should always be avoided. In fact, manifestations of conflict of interests in research are serious misconducts, which damage the image of the agent and the organization in which she operates. Sometimes this reputation damage may even be caused by an *apparent conflict of interests*, which should also be avoided. An apparent conflict is a situation in which, although the secondary interest of the agent does not interfere with the primary, a reasonable external subject might think, or might suspect, that an interference exists, and therefore the professional judgment is likely to be compromised. The reason to avoid even apparent conflict of interests is just to avoid any damage of reputation. An example of a policy that defines conflict of interests is presented in Box 6.2.

Confidentiality is another key ethically sensitive issue in research. Researchers very often are exposed to confidential information, and it is expected that they keep it confidential, not only avoiding any deliberate disclosure, but also protecting the information from any possible access by unauthorized individuals. For example, a paper submitted for publication must be kept by a reviewer as confidential information. It should never be copied and distributed to others. It should also be kept in places that cannot be accessed by others. To protect the parties involved and precisely define roles and responsibilities, confidentiality terms are often explicitly stated. Box 6.3 illustrates an example of a confidentiality policy concerning research publications.

Researchers are often involved in evaluations and decisions. Ethical principles demand for *fair judgement*. Evaluation and decision may refer to a paper submitted for publication, or a researcher being considered for hiring or promotion, or a research proposal submitted for funding. Fair judgement means that the individual

> ## Box 6.2: An Example Policy for Conflict of Interests in Research
>
> The following excerpt is quoted from the Conflict of Interest (COI) Policy for ACM Publications.[2]
>
> The following are considered to be specific exemplars of relationships that produce COIs. Individuals in such relationships should not be involved in peer review of, or making editorial decisions about, ACM published materials provided by the related parties.
>
> - Notable personal or professional rivalry/animosity (publicly known or not)
> - The lifelong relationship between Ph.D. student and Ph.D. supervisor
> - Personal or family relationships that would reasonably cause others to doubt impartiality.
> - Potential for financial gain or significant recognition, personally or for a close associate or family member
> - Within the last 2 years or reasonably expected within the next year:
>   - Working closely together (e.g., at the same institution, company or organization; or within the same organizational team)
>   - Supervisor/Supervisee relationship exists
>   - Funder or program manager/awardee relationship exists
>   - Recipients of joint funding or significant professional collaboration
>   - Joint authorship of an archival publication (e.g., an item having a DOI)

involved in the evaluation should be objective and should not be biased by prejudice, personal interests, preferences, and beliefs. For example, a paper should receive fair treatment also in the case it does not follow the mainstream approaches that are currently hot in a given area. Judgement should never be biased by gender, country, institution, or any other personal information about the individuals associated with the subject being evaluated. In the case of comparative judgement, fairness also means uniformity of the evaluation criteria and of the mindset across all subjects.

So far in this discussion I focused on ethical issues arising in the relations among individuals involved in research. Researchers should behave ethically also with respect to the research community. We observed that the research community is by and large self-managed by researchers. Relations rely on cooperation, personal integrity, and trust. Researchers have an obligation to sustain the research community not only by contributing to advancing their own research, but also ensuring that new generations of researchers are formed, diffusing results and making them available for further advances, reviewing others' work, and so on. Proper balance between effort allocation in own research and service to the community can vary across individuals, and in particular it varies according to seniority. But denying any kind of support to community activities is a misconduct.

---

[2]https://www.acm.org/publications/policies/conflict-of-interest.

6.3   Ethical Principles in the Practice of Research

In this section I revisit the general principles of research ethics by discussing how and where they arise in the various activities in which scientists may be engaged in their daily practice. I also introduce additional ethical concerns that are specific to certain activities. We have seen that in many cases the answers to the ethical questions arising while doing research cannot be reduced to straightforward binary choices between what is right and what is wrong. Ethics can seldom be reduced to just an exhaustive list of obligations and rights, to-do's and not-to-do's. The ethical space in which researchers operate is not binary, but continuous, ranging from clearly unethical to acceptable conducts. Behaving ethically means deciding responsibly after honestly and carefully scrutinizing whether a conduct may endanger integrity. In unclear situations, is advisable to reason in a consequence-oriented manner, focusing on maximizing or promoting the collective advancement of research and, ultimately, societal welfare. In case of doubt, it is wise to follow the safest route that minimizes the risks.

Box 6.3: An Example Policy for Confidentiality in Research Publications

Hereafter, I briefly comment the document "Policy on Roles and Responsibilities in ACM Publishing" by the ACM.[3] The document contains the following statement:

> When an author makes a submission, a confidential review process is initiated. Reviewers can expect ACM to acknowledge their efforts in the publication process, while maintaining confidentiality of the submissions they reviewed.

Notice that this statement is to protect reviewers. The next statements instead describe obligations by the reviewers to protect authors:

> ACM expects reviewers to comply with several obligations:
>
> - Maintain the confidentiality of the existence and status of submissions of which the reviewer becomes aware.
> - Not use results from submitted works in their works, research or grant proposals, unless and until that material appears in other publicly available formats, such as a technical report or as a published work.
> - Not distribute a submission to anyone unless approved by the editor handling the submission.
> - Maintain the anonymity of the other reviewers, should they become known to that reviewer.
> - Breach of confidentiality by one of the parties involved is especially bad because others rely on the assurance that the information they provide is not shared without their consent.

---

[3]https://www.acm.org/publications/policies/roles-and-responsibilities.

Let us first focus on the stage in which a research is carried out. Researchers have an obligation to know the area in which they work and which contributions have been given previously by others, to honestly place their contribution in the proper context. They should give credit and not pretend unjustified novelty of their contribution. Appropriation of others' ideas or results without giving appropriate record and with the intention that they be taken as own work is ethically unacceptable. Researchers should also never give unjustified negative credit to others' work, dismissing or criticizing it unfairly, to shed a better light on their own contribution.

When it comes to publication, researchers should make sure that the papers they write does not contain discriminating statements (for example, with respect to gender, religion, political, or social groups, and so on). Researchers must watch for text plagiarism (including self-plagiarism). In addition to misconducts, there are bad practices that should be avoided, like the mentioned search for the least-publishable unit, which leads to the deplorable proliferation of papers providing negligible contributions. Flooding the community with too many papers of little relevance is bad, distracts researchers from focusing on interesting problems, and abuses reviewers' time. This goes hand-in-hand with the unjustified proliferation of new journals and conferences, whose scientific quality is often, at best, questionable. Researchers should carefully avoid any endorsement of these deplorable practices. They should not submit contributions and should decline editorial responsibility for publications of dubious scientific stand. This is even more necessary for predatory publishers!

Double submission is another serious publication misconduct. It can be defined as the submission of a paper for publication (in a journal or in refereed conference proceedings) while it is under concurrent submission to another publication. The practice of double submission is considered unethical because it wastes the time of editors, peer reviewers, and (potentially) readers. Submitting an extended version of a conference paper to an archival journal, with proper explanation to the editors and the reviewers, is instead legitimate. Resubmission to a new venue of a paper that was previously rejected by another is also legitimate. It is bad, however, not to take into serious consideration possible comments from the original reviewers in the preparation of the manuscript for the second submission. One should also consider that an original reviewer might be asked to review the new submission. She would rightly feel offended if her criticisms and suggestions for improvement of the original submission were completely ignored by the authors.

Another ethical issue concerning publication is: who should be listed as a co-author? The answer is: all those who contributed. Deliberately omitting an individual who provided substantial contribution is unethical, as would be listing as an author someone who has not contributed. Deciding what makes a contribution substantial may in same cases raise questions (for example, in the case of large projects). There are also cultural differences that may affect this decisions. In certain very traditional and hierarchically structured organizations, the normal practice is that the head of a scientific group co-authors all contributions of the researchers in the group. The prevalent accepted practice, however, is that only those who directly contributed to the work should sign it. Listing as an author someone who gave no contribution, only as a personal favor (for example, to help in a promotion case or to boost a colleague's CV) would instead be unethical.

A related problem concerns the ordering of the author list. In some cases, which may depend on the tradition in a field or on the local culture, the ordering of authors is not significant; the authors are listed in alphabetic order, assuming that they all equally contributed to the paper.[4] In other cases, the first author is the researcher who has made the most significant intellectual contribution to the work. This is also reflected by the common practice of referring to a paper by the first author's name; e.g., "XXX et al. report that ... " In certain areas the implicit convention is that the most important author, in terms of seniority or responsibility in the research, is the last of the list. From an ethical standpoint, it is advisable to follow the convention adopted by the specific research field to list the authors, if there is one. In the absence of a clear rule indicating who mainly contributed to a paper, all co-authors should be considered as equal contributors. The problem of paper authorship is a special case of the more general problem of proper attributing intellectual property of research results. Because scientific research may lead to results that have practical value, intellectual property is a legal right to control the application of an idea in a specific context (through a patent) or control the expression of an idea (through a copyright). It is very important that all researchers who contributed substantially to the idea participate in its exploitation.

When a paper is published, it may happen that it contains mistakes that went undetected in the review process. When researchers become aware of that, they should not ignore or hide them, but they should instead make public statements, for example in their web site and (or) by submitting a correction to the journal, acknowledging the mistake.

Ethical issues also arise in paper reviewing. As I repeatedly observed, accepting to review is a community service. When asked to review a paper, one should dismiss the request only if there are objective reasons. If one accepts, time and effort should be allocated to this crucial task. The provided review report must be detailed, constructive, rigorous, and avoid bias with respect to the authors (if their identity is disclosed), and with respect to the subject. Reviewers should treat the paper as confidential information and should review it fairly: breaking confidentiality and fairness are serious misconducts.

Publication may also be affected by conflict of interests due to the author/reviewer relationship. For example, they may be relatives, they may members of the same research group, they had a recent research collaboration, they belong to the same department, one is or was a PhD student of the other, and so on. Occurrence of a conflict of interests is a serious misconduct. Whenever one submits a paper or is asked to review a paper, one should always watch for possible insurgence of

---

[4]This convention is sometimes broken to give special recognition to one of the authors, who is listed first.

conflicts of interests. Very often, they are explicitly stated, but in case of doubt one should explicitly raise the potential problem upfront.

Confidentiality, fairness, and freedom from conflict of interests are key ethical principles also when researchers are engaged in evaluation of individuals (progress of a PhD student, hiring or promoting researchers) and evaluation of research projects for funding.

Proper management of research funding raises an additional specific ethical issue. Funding money must be used wisely and according to the scope for which one has been funded. Public funding comes from taxpayers and is allocated to advance the frontiers of knowledge and address societal problems. Any misuse of research money destroys trust and shakes the public confidence in the integrity of science.

Boxes 6.4 and 6.5 discuss concrete examples of practical situations in ethical issues arise. Box 6.4 discusses review delegation by a senior researcher to a junior collaborator. Box 6.5 concerns disclosure of a successful research proposal to a potential new applicant.

As a last point, what happens if one witnesses an objective, serious violation to ethical standards? One should not become a partner in misconduct, because it weakens the health of self-regulating research processes. Institutions have procedures in place to investigate, report, and react objectively, firmly, and unemotionally to serious misconducts. One should report to them, adopting the necessary confidentiality precautions.

6.4 Topic Specific Ethical Issues

In this section, I discuss when and how the specific subject being investigated, or the research method being followed, raise ethical issues that must be carefully examined by the researcher and may require special actions. This concern is traditionally well understood in the case of medical research, which often involves human participants. The ethical implications of research involving human subjects can also be relevant in social sciences. Physicists have long been debating the ethical implications of research that can lead to the development of mass destruction weapons. Today, ethical issues increasingly arise in almost all research areas, for two main reasons. First, transition from research to technology and innovation occurs at an increasingly high speed, before researchers have made any attempt to think of, or anticipate, the possible ethical consequences of its use. Second, technological developments more and more directly involve and affect humans, in their private life, in relation with other humans, with society, and with the physical environment. Researchers can no longer ignore that their work can have ethical implications.

The debate on the possible ethical implications of a specific research has often originated heated discussions among scientists. It exploded at the end of World War II, when physicists started passionate discussions on the relation between research and war. The scientific contributions of eminent physicists in the Manhattan Project led to the development of the nuclear bomb, which ended the war and also caused

Box 6.4: Can Review Assignments be Transferred to Others?

Alice is a senior scientist and she is a member of the program committee of a conference. When she receives her set of papers to review, she realizes that she underestimated the review effort. Because of other commitments she accepted meanwhile, Alice decides to delegate all the reviews to her junior collaborators (two PhD students and a post-doc). She passes the reviews they write on her behalf on to the program committee without even looking at them, since she trusts her collaborators.

Mark is also a member of the program committee of the same conference. When he receives the papers assigned for review, he realizes that some of them fall in the specific research areas of two of his PhD students. He believes that it is very important for PhD students to learn how to do peer review. Therefore he delegates the review of the papers to the students, does a quick sanity check of the reports they write, and submits them to the program committee under his name.

Mary is in exactly the same situation as Mark. She passes on the papers for review to the PhD students, but she goes through their reports, discusses and revises with them both the text and the final recommendation. Eventually, Mary and the PhD students reach a shared evaluation of the work, which is submitted to the program committee, along with the names of all the reviewers.

Of the three cases, the first is an example of a misconduct. When Alice accepted to be a member of the program committee, she committed to personally review the papers assigned to her. By offloading her job to others, she seriously broke her commitment. Delegation of the review might be an infringement of confidentiality. A conference may allow the committee member to nominate a sub-reviewer, but the sub-reviewer—as the name clearly indicates—is subordinate to the main reviewer, who has to take the final responsibility for the review. Mark's case raises similar problems (delegation of a job that cannot be delegated and possible infringement of confidentiality), although he was driven by a good motivation (exposing PhD students to peer review). Finally, Mary's case does not raise any ethical concerns, assuming that the conference explicitly authorizes committee members to choose sub-reviewers. Mary demonstrates special attention in educating her students to become conscientious reviewers.

> **Box 6.5: Can a Successful Research Proposal be Shared with Potential New Applicants?**
>
> Alex is going to apply for funding to a prestigious, very selective program dedicated to young researchers. His past PhD advisor, Michael, chaired the selection committee the previous year for the same funding program. Alex asks Michael some advice on how to best structure his application to make it successful. Michael decides to share confidentially with Alex a copy of a successful past application as a source of inspiration.
>
> This story shows an example of a misconduct. Research proposals are known to reviewers under confidential terms that in no way are transferable to others. Michael could have given personal advice to Alex without breaking confidentiality. He could have suggested Alex to contact personally one of the successful applicants asking for further advice. Suppose that Alex knows well Susan, one of the past successful applicants. He might ask her confidentially if she is willing to share her application as a source of inspiration. This alternative course of actions would be acceptable.

mass destruction. At the same time, in 1945 in Nuremberg, Germany, a series of trials were held against war criminals. In one of the trials, German medical doctors responsible for conducting inhumane, unethical medical experiments on prisoners in concentration camps were tried. One of the results of the discussions around the trial was the development of a ten-point document, known as Nuremberg Code, which states the conditions for legitimate medical research. This document is considered as a landmark in the history of medical research ethics, and had a massive influence on global human rights, recognizing autonomy and dignity of human subjects as well as the principles of harm avoidance and respect.

The notion of *informed and uncoerced consent* is the cornerstone of the Nuremberg Code, and since then it became a cornerstone of ethical research involving humans. This is the given definition:

> The voluntary consent of the human subject is absolutely essential. This means that the person involved should have legal capacity to give consent; should be so situated as to be able to exercise free power of choice, and should have sufficient knowledge and comprehension of the subject matter involved as to enable him to make an understanding and enlightened decision.

According to this definition, consent validity requires (1) competence and capacity, (2) adequate information, and (3) voluntariness. This concept is now assumed as a standard ethical requirement for any kind of research that involves humans, not only medical, but also social and technological research.

Further ethical issues arise if research involves vulnerable and/or non-competent subjects. There may be a need for research to involve these kinds of subjects, such as children, for example to study their behavior and their learning progress in special circumstances, like interaction with technological devices. Likewise, technology could bring tremendous benefits to impaired individuals. Researchers must be aware of the need to offer special protection to vulnerable participants, both in the development of the research and in its potential subsequent exploitation. In the example of children, informed consent may be expressed by parents. In the case of impaired adults, it may be a legal tutor.

The principles of privacy and confidentiality also raise key ethical issues. The two terms are often used interchangeably, although they are related, but not equivalent, concepts. *Privacy* refers to the right to control access to oneself. It includes physical privacy, such as ensuring that curtains are closed during physical examinations, and information privacy, ensuring that personal information only flows through enforceable privacy principles. *Confidentiality* refers to information only. For example, the legal duty of confidentiality obliges health care practitioners to protect their patients against inappropriate disclosure of personal health information.

Research can raise privacy and confidentiality concerns. For example, a research on how programmers' productivity varies depending on previous experience in a given programming language should never allow one to trace productivity data to a specific individual involved in experiments. Likewise, a research on the effect of alcohol assumption and fertility of adult males should never allow identification of a specific participant in the experiment. The key techniques used here are data protection and data anonymization.

The General Data Protection Regulation (GDPR) issued by the European Union, in operation since 2018, regulates data protection and privacy for all individuals within the EU. It is perhaps the most advanced case of legislation that protects citizens, who are increasingly exposed to threats due to pervasive information technology. Researchers operating in Europe are required to be compliant with the GDPR in their research activities.

Most research institutions promote adoption of ethical research methods and provide an institutional review board, also known as *ethics committee*, whose mandate is to review ethics-sensitive research proposals submitted by researchers, to approve (or reject) them, and to monitor their advances. The main purpose is to assure that appropriate steps are taken to protect the rights and welfare of humans participating as subjects in a research study. It may also watch for ethical participation of animals or ethical effects on the environment, whenever these apply. Approval from the ethics committee is normally a required prerequisite for ethically sensitive research proposals submitted for research funding. Almost all countries have regulations or guidelines governing human subject studies and ethics committees oversee them. However, the organizational responsibilities and the scope of the oversight purview can differ substantially.

6.5   Digital Ethics

In the nineteenth and in the twentieth century, automation has been progressively applied to industry, replacing manual, repetitive tasks and gaining efficiency. In the twenty-first century, it is more and more applied to tasks that require intellectual skills, interacting with humans in various ways and often replacing them. Digital technology has invaded both the private sphere and human relations with the external world. Humans increasingly interact and cooperate in the digital space. The space in which they live became *cyber-physical* and the boundaries between the digital and the physical worlds is blurring. In addition, algorithms may take the form of digital individuals which populate our world, with whom we constantly interact. Digital agents not only help humans, supporting them in complex decisions, but can directly decide on their behalf, and automated decisions may affect other humans.

Decisions made by algorithms are mainly based on predictions about the subject matter concerning the decision, based on what a computing engine has learnt from past data about the same subject matter. For example, a judge may delegate decisions to digital peers, which may sentence a criminal based on her likelihood of reoffending, computed by a predictive "intelligent" algorithm. Likewise, a doctor may delegate the choice of the best cancer treatment for a patient to a digital cancer specialist. New ethical problems arise, which concern the definition of what is a "proper behavior" in the cyber-physical world and, in particular, what is the role of algorithmic decisions by algorithms. Society is increasingly concerned with the need to guarantee that scientific and technological progress proceed in accordance with human values and needs. For more discussion of these issues, the reader may refer to [8, 24, 32, 64].

Progress in scientific research is now challenging the very notions of intelligence, and even the unique role of humans in developing new knowledge and dominating the world. The debate has reached unprecedented levels of controversy in the recent years, and is likely to be a dominant discussion in the future. The debate is engaging scientists from all areas and very different backgrounds, ranging from Informatics to Physical Sciences and Engineering, to Life Sciences, Social Sciences, Philosophy, and Law. It is not only happening within closed, specialized circles, but has also reached the general public, engaging scientists in necessary, yet critical, outreaching activities. A discussion of these challenges is very relevant to the topics discussed in this book, and cannot be ignored. At the same time, the discussion is still in a rather premature stage and has not led to generally accepted conclusions that could be distilled in a consolidated and coherent set of results. Hereafter I only address a few points. I also mainly focus on the implications of the discussion on the role of machine intelligence in research.

The notion of intelligence has been discussed by scientists and philosophers throughout history. The notion of machine intelligence is also elusive and generated heated debates since the seminal work by Alan Turing [60] in 1950. A few years later, John McCarthy coined the term *artificial intelligence* and laid its foundations. Among other things, intelligence includes two capacities that are key to scientific research: rationality and creativity. The questions arising from recent advances of science concern the role of artificial intelligence in producing research. Machines can definitely *reason* rationally, and in many cases they even surpass humans in quality and performance. The key question is whether they can act creatively.

Creativity—the basic instinct that drives research—has also been studied for many years, especially by cognitive scientists. Margaret Boden [5] is well known for her studies on creativity. She distinguishes among three different types of creativity, called combinatorial, exploratory, and transformational, which differ in the psychological processes involved in generating new ideas.

Combinatorial creativity involves the generation of novel and interesting combinations of known ideas. One does not expect X to be combined with Y, which are normally regarded as mutually irrelevant. Yet their combination generates surprises. We already examined cases where research in one area has been transferred into a completely different area generating unexpected good results. As another example, researchers have been studying bio-inspired algorithms, which provide automated solutions to practical problems, inspired by biological behaviors. Solutions proved to be quite effective in many cases. Specifically, optimization problems have been solved by reproducing the pheromone-based communication of biological ants into computer algorithms [10]. The creative act in these studies consisted in conjoining ideas from natural science (how ant colonies behave) and algorithms, to spawn a new research area, called *ant colony optimization*.

Explorative creativity consists of exploring the extensions of known knowledge. It corresponds to incremental creation, and perhaps it is the prevalent creative process in science. Philosopher of science Thomas Kuhn called it *normal science* [31] (see also Box 2.5). Explorative creativity is perhaps the prevalent manifestation of creativity in research, which guarantees continuous progress.

Transformational creativity is the most elusive kind of creativity, which generates discontinuity in scientific progress. As an example taken from music, instead of science, one can think of the radical departure from tonal music done by composers like Arnold Schoenberg, Alban Berg, and Anton Webern, who composed music using all twelve tones of the chromatic scale in such a way that they are "equal", i.e. having no tonic, no dominant, no major or minor keys, and hence no distinction between harmony and dissonance. According to Kuhn, transformational creativity generates paradigm shifts. It leads to *revolutionary science*, which brings groundbreaking results and opens new research avenues.

While machines can be designed to achieve certain kinds of explorative and combinatorial creativity, it is unlikely that they will ever be able to exhibit transformational creativity. Machine intelligence should be viewed as complementary to human intelligence. It can be a tremendously effective aid for humans in doing research. Understanding how machine and human intelligence can effectively cooperate in doing scientific research is an open challenge that needs to be addressed and may bring to new exciting developments in the future.

Research generates fantastic new opportunities, but also potential risks that are difficult to predict, especially due to the speed of continuous generation of innovations into the social fabric. This is placing responsibilities on researchers, who are asked to shape science and technology in accordance with human values and needs, instead of allowing science and technology to shape humans.

Before concluding, I would like to discuss the ethical implications of research by looking at a paradigmatic case of technological research: the development of autonomous vehicles, such as driverless cars. One might look at this as an example of purely technological research, and perhaps researchers may take this approach and just focus on the technological challenges involved. The research, however, has profound ethical implications. On the one end, it may be viewed as a solution for the good of humans: it liberates them from a boring task like driving and reduces the risks of accidents due to driver failures (for example, the driver falls asleep, or is drunk). At the same time, the researcher must realize that the automated control system being designed has to make ethical decisions. If a child suddenly crosses an intersection when the light is red and the car enters the intersection at a speed such that the only two alternatives are (1) invest the child, or (2) avoid entering the intersection by crashing against a guardrail, which alternative should be chosen? Potentially kill the child (who is in fault) or potentially kill the passengers in the car? This example is a rather extreme case, where there is no easy nor obvious solution to the ethical issue raised by research. The problem, however, cannot be ignored and decisions need to be made. Similar ethical issues arise in cases of *dual-use research*, meaning that a research has the potential to be used for both good and bad ends. It is important to identify and counter bad ends before the research produces results, and not after. For example, suppose that a social media researcher works on a new advanced platform: ethics-informed research would also focus on identification of possible misuses and possible prevention mechanisms.

I would like to end our discussion on research ethics by stressing again that research ethics cannot be reduced to a to-do list. There are general ethical principles, but their application is not straightforward. Rather it requires careful investigation and honest assumption of active, personal responsibility by the researcher.

6.6   Further Reading

A report on responsible conduct in research has been issued by the Committee on Science, Engineering, and Public Policy of the USA National Academy of Sciences, National Academy of Engineering, and Institute of Medicine [50]. A reference on ethics in research has also been delivered by the European Commission [66]. All European academies produced a short, yet very informative, booklet [3].

Bertrand Meyer in [36] revisits ethical principles from the standpoint of a researcher in Informatics. He argues for rational application of a few well-defined concepts in a well-defined scope to operationalize ethics into practical decisions. Jeroen van den Hoven in [23] argues that our traditional attempts to deal with ethical issues in the digital age are inevitably too late or too slow; they should instead be anticipated in the conception of innovation.

Ethics in Informatics is discussed by Deborah Johnson [25]. For an introduction to the ethical issues in computing, see also the textbook by Joseph M. Kizza [27].

References

1. ACM: Artifact review and badging URL https://www.acm.org/publications/policies/artifact-review-badging
2. Adler, R., Ewing, J., Taylor, P.: Citation statistics: A report from the international mathematical union (imu) in cooperation with the international council of industrial and applied mathematics (iciam) and the institute of mathematical statistics (ims). Statistical Science **24**(1), 1–14 (2009). URL http://www.jstor.org/stable/20697661
3. ALLEA: The European code of conduct for research integrity, revised edition (2017). URL https://www.allea.org/wp-content/uploads/2017/05/ALLEA-European-Code-of-Conduct-for-Research-Integrity-2017.pdf
4. Berlin, I.: The Hedgehog and the Fox: An Essay on Tolstoy's View of History. Elephant paperbacks. Ivan R. Dee, Publisher (1993)
5. Boden, M.A.: The Creative Mind: Myths and Mechanisms. Basic Books, Inc., New York, NY, USA (1991)
6. Carayannis, E., Campbell, D.: Mode 3 knowledge production in quadruple helix innovation systems. In: E. Carayannis, D. Campbell (eds.) Mode 3 Knowledge Production in Quadruple Helix Innovation Systems: 21st-Century Democracy, Innovation, and Entrepreneurship for Development. SpringerBriefs in Business, New York, NY (2012)
7. De Millo, R.A., Lipton, R.J., Perlis, A.J.: Social processes and proofs of theorems and programs. Commun. ACM **22**(5), 271–280 (1979). https://doi.org/10.1145/359104.359106. URL http://doi.acm.org/10.1145/359104.359106
8. DIGHUM: Vienna Manifesto on Digital Humanism (2019). URL https://www.informatik.tuwien.ac.at/dighum/manifesto/
9. Dodig Crnkovic, G.: Constructive research and info-computational knowledge generation. In: L. Magnani, W. Carnielli, C. Pizzi (eds.) Model-Based Reasoning in Science and Technology, vol. 314, pp. 359–380. Springer, Berlin, Heidelberg
10. Dorigo, M., Birattari, M., Stützle, T.: Ant colony optimization. Computational Intelligence Magazine, IEEE **1**, 28–39 (2006). https://doi.org/10.1109/MCI.2006.329691
11. Esposito, F., Ghezzi, C., Hermenegildo, M., Kirchner, H., Ong, L.: Informatics Research Evaluation. Informatics Europe (2018). URL https://www.informatics-europe.org/publications.html
12. Etzkowitz, H., Leydesdorff, L.: The triple helix – university-industry-government relations: A laboratory for knowledge based economic development. EASST Review **14**(1), 14–19 (1995)
13. Feibelman, P.: A PhD Is Not Enough!: A Guide to Survival in Science. ReadHowYouWant.com, Limited (2011)
14. Feyerabend, P.: Against Method. Verso (1993)
15. Feynman, R., Davies, P.: The Character of Physical Law. Penguin Books Limited (2007)

16. Friedman, B., Schneider, F.B.: Incentivizing quality and impact: Evaluating scholarship in hiring, tenure, and promotion. Computing Research Association (2016). URL https://cra.org/resources/best-practice-memos/incentivizing-quality-and-impact-evaluating-scholarship-in-hiring-tenure-and-promotion/

17. Godfrey-Smith, P.: Theory and Reality: An Introduction to the Philosophy of Science. University of Chicago Press, Chicago (2003)

18. Gosling, P., Noordam, L.: Mastering Your PhD: Survival and Success in the Doctoral Years and Beyond. Springer Berlin Heidelberg (2006)

19. Harari, Y.: Sapiens: A Brief History of Humankind. Random House (2014). URL https://books.google.it/books?id=1EiJAwAAQBAJ

20. Harari, Y.: Homo Deus: A Brief History of Tomorrow. Random House (2016). URL https://books.google.it/books?id=dWYyCwAAQBAJ

21. Hicks, D., Wouters, P., Waltman, L., de Rijcke, S., Rafols, I.: Bibliometrics: The leiden manifesto for research metrics. Nature News **520**(7548), 429 (2015). https://doi.org/10.1038/520429a. URL http://www.nature.com/news/bibliometrics-the-leiden-manifesto-for-research-metrics-1.17351

22. Hopcroft, J.E., Motwani, R., Ullman, J.D.: Introduction to Automata Theory, Languages, and Computation (3rd Edition). Addison-Wesley Longman Publishing Co., Inc., USA (2006)

23. van den Hoven, J.: Ethics for the digital age: Where are the moral specs? In: H. Werthner, F. van Harmelen (eds.) Informatics in the Future, pp. 65–76. Springer International Publishing, Cham (2017)

24. Inverardi, P.: The European perspective on responsible computing. Commun. ACM **62**(4), 64–64 (2019). https://doi.org/10.1145/3311783. URL http://doi.acm.org/10.1145/3311783

25. Johnson, D.G.: Computer Ethics, 4th edn. Prentice Hall Press, USA (2009)

26. Kearns, H., Gardiner, M.: The care and maintenance of your adviser. Nature **469**, 570 (2011). https://doi.org/10.1038/nj7331-570a

27. Kizza, J.M.: Ethical and Secure Computing - A Concise Module, Second Edition. Undergraduate Topics in Computer Science. Springer (2019). https://doi.org/10.1007/978-3-030-03937-0

28. Kramer, J.: Is abstraction the key to computing? Commun. ACM **50**(4), 36–42 (2007). URL https://doi.org/10.1145/1232743.1232745

29. Krishnamurthi, S., Vitek, J.: The real software crisis: Repeatability as a core value. Commun. ACM **58**(3), 34–36 (2015). https://doi.org/10.1145/2658987. URL http://doi.acm.org/10.1145/2658987

30. Kuhn, T.: The Copernican Revolution: Planetary Astronomy in the Development of Western Thought. A Harvard Paperback. Harvard University Press (1957)

31. Kuhn, T.S.: The Structure of Scientific Revolutions. University of Chicago Press, Chicago (1962)

32. Larus, J., Hankin, C., Carson, S.G., Christen, M., Crafa, S., Grau, O., Kirchner, C., Knowles, B., McGettrick, A., Tamburri, D.A., Werthner, H.: When Computers Decide: European Recommendations on Machine-Learned Automated Decision Making. Informatics Europe and EU ACM (2018). URL https://www.informatics-europe.org/publications.html

33. Medawar, P.: The Art of the Soluble. Methuen (1967)

34. Medawar, P.: Advice To A Young Scientist. Alfred P. Sloan Foundation series. Basic Books (2008)

35. Meyer, B.: Incremental research vs. paradigm-shift mania. Commun. ACM **55**(9), 8–9 (2012). URL https://doi.org/10.1145/2330667.2330670

36. Meyer, B.: Rational ethics. In: H. Werthner, F. van Harmelen (eds.) Informatics in the Future, pp. 49–64. Springer International Publishing, Cham (2017)

37. OECD: Frascati Manual. OECD Publishing (2015). https://doi.org/10.1787/9789264239012-en. URL https://www.oecd-ilibrary.org/content/publication/9789264239012-en

38. Offit, P.A.: Bad Advice: Or Why Celebrities, Politicians, and Activists Aren't Your Best Source of Health Information. Columbia University Press (2018). URL http://www.jstor.org/stable/10.7312/offi18698

39. Parnas, D.L.: Stop the numbers game. Commun. ACM **50**(11), 19–21 (2007). https://doi.org/10.1145/1297797.1297815. URL http://doi.acm.org/10.1145/1297797.1297815
40. Patterson, D., Snyder, L., Ullman, J.: Evaluating computer scientists and engineers for promotion and tenure. Computing Research Association (1999). URL https://cra.org/resources/best-practice-memos/incentivizing-quality-and-impact-evaluating-scholarship-in-hiring-tenure-and-promotion/
41. Patterson, D.A.: Viewpoint: Your students are your legacy. Commun. ACM **52**(3), 30–33 (2009). https://doi.org/10.1145/1467247.1467259. URL http://doi.acm.org/10.1145/1467247.1467259
42. Plowright, D.: Charles Sanders Peirce: Pragmatism and Education. SpringerBriefs in Education. Springer Netherlands (2015). URL https://books.google.it/books?id=5vcUCwAAQBAJ
43. Popper, K.R.: The Logic of Scientific Discovery. Routledge (1959)
44. Pruzan, P.: Research Methodology: The Aims, Practices and Ethics of Science. Springer International Publishing (2016)
45. Ramsey, N.: Learn technical writing in two hours per week (2006). URL https://www.cs.tufts.edu/~nr/pubs/two-abstract.html
46. REF2019/2: Panel criteria and working methods (2019). URL https://www.ref.ac.uk/media/1084/ref-2019_02-panel-criteria-and-working-methods.pdf
47. European Commission Directorate General for Research & Innovation: H2020 Programme – Guidelines to the Rules on Open Access to Scientific Publications and Open Access to Research Data in Horizon 2020 (2017). URL http://ec.europa.eu/research/participants/data/ref/h2020/grants_manual/hi/oa_pilot/h2020-hi-oa-pilot-guide_en.pdf
48. Russell, B.: The Problems of Philosophy. Hackett classics. Hackett Publishing Company (1990). URL https://books.google.it/books?id=ZNid1isYIncC
49. Saenen, B., Borrell-Damian, L.: Reflections on University Research Assessment: key concepts, issues and actors. European University Association (2019). URL https://eua.eu/component/attachments/attachments.html?id=2144
50. National Academies of Sciences, National Academies of Engineering, Institute of Medicine: On Being a Scientist: A Guide to Responsible Conduct in Research: Third Edition. The National Academies Press, Washington, DC, USA (2009). https://doi.org/10.17226/12192
51. Senor, D., Singer, S.: Start-Up Nation: The Story of Israel's Economic Miracle. McClelland & Stewart, Toronto, Canada (2011)
52. Sigmund, K.: Exact Thinking in Demented Times: The Vienna Circle and the Epic Quest for the Foundations of Science. Basic Books, Inc., New York, NY, USA (2017)
53. Smith, P.: Einstein. Life & Times. Haus Publishing (2005). URL https://books.google.it/books?id=5VcrDwAAQBAJ
54. Stokes, D.E.: Pasteur's Quadrant: Basic Science and Technological Innovation. Brookings Institution Press, Washington, D.C. (1997)
55. Strunk, W., White, E.: The Elements of Style. Longman (2009)
56. Suber, P.: Open Access. The MIT Press (2012)
57. Tedre, M.: The Science of Computing: Shaping a Discipline. Chapman & Hall/CRC (2014)
58. Thompson, J.: Advice to a young researcher: With reminiscences of a life in science. Philosophical transactions. Series A, Mathematical, physical, and engineering sciences **371**(1993) (2013). https://doi.org/10.1098/rsta.2012.0449
59. Thurston, R.H.: The growth of the steam engine. Popular Science Monthly **12** (1877)
60. Turing, A.: Computing machinery and intelligence. Mind **59**, 433–460 (1950)
61. Turner, R.: Computational Artifacts: Towards a Philosophy of Computer Science, 1st edn. Springer Publishing Company, Incorporated (2018)
62. Ullman, J.D.: Viewpoint: Advising students for success. Commun. ACM **52**(3), 34–37 (2009). https://doi.org/10.1145/1467247.1467260. URL http://doi.acm.org/10.1145/1467247.1467260
63. Vardi, M.Y.: The long game of research. Commun. ACM **62**(9), 7–7 (2019). https://doi.org/10.1145/3352489. URL http://doi.acm.org/10.1145/3352489
64. Vardi, M.Y.: To serve humanity. Commun. ACM **62**(7), 7–7 (2019). https://doi.org/10.1145/3338092. URL http://doi.acm.org/10.1145/3338092

65. Wieringa, R.J.: Design science methodology for information systems and software engineering. Springer (2014). https://doi.org/10.1007/978-3-662-43839-8
66. Wrigley, A., Hughes, J., Sheehan, M., Wilkinson, S., Hunter, D.: European Textbook on Ethics in Research (2010). https://doi.org/10.2777/51536
67. Zobel, J.: Writing for Computer Science, 3rd edn. Springer Publishing Company, Incorporated (2015)

CPSIA information can be obtained
at www.ICGtesting.com
Printed in the USA
LVHW011408130720
660451LV00001B/88

9 783030 451561